Recipes: A Quintet of Cuisines

Contents

Illustrations:

Foods of the World

TIME-LIFE BOOKS, NEW YORK

Egg and Cheese Dishes

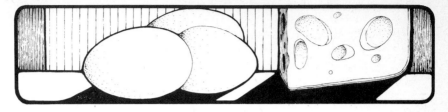

Fondue Neuchâteloise (Switzerland)

To serve 4 to 6

½ pound imported Swiss Gruyère cheese, coarsely grated (about 2 cups)
½ pound imported Swiss Emmentaler cheese, coarsely grated (about 2 cups)
1 tablespoon cornstarch
2 cups dry white wine, preferably Neuchâtel
1 medium-sized garlic clove, peeled and bruised with the flat of a knife
2 tablespoons imported kirsch
⅛ teaspoon nutmeg, preferably freshly grated
⅛ teaspoon salt
Freshly ground black pepper
1 large loaf French or Italian bread with the crust left on, cut into 1-inch cubes

In a large bowl, toss together the cheeses and cornstarch until thoroughly combined. Pour the wine into a 2-quart fondue dish (or any 2-quart flame-proof enameled casserole), drop in the garlic, and bring to a boil over high heat. Let the wine boil briskly for 1 or 2 minutes, then with a slotted spoon remove and discard the garlic. Lower the heat so that the wine barely simmers. Stirring constantly with a table fork, add the cheese mixture a handful at a time, letting each handful melt before adding another. When the fondue is creamy and smooth, stir in the kirsch, nutmeg, salt and a few grindings of black pepper, and taste for seasoning.

To serve, place the fondue dish or casserole over an alcohol or gas table burner in the center of the dining table, regulating the heat so that the fondue barely simmers. Set a basketful of the bread cubes alongside the fondue. Traditionally, each diner spears a cube of bread on a fork (preferably a long-handled fondue fork), swirls the bread about in the fondue until it is thoroughly coated, then eats it immediately.

Délices de Fromage (Switzerland)
DEEP-FRIED CHEESE SQUARES

To make about 12 squares

4 tablespoons unsalted butter
1¼ cups all-purpose flour
1½ cups milk
3 egg yolks
1 teaspoon salt
⅛ teaspoon white pepper
1 cup freshly grated imported Swiss
Gruyère cheese (about ¼ pound)
1 cup freshly grated imported Swiss
Emmentaler cheese (about ¼ pound)
2 eggs beaten together with ⅓ cup milk
1 cup dried bread crumbs
Vegetable oil for deep frying

In a heavy 3- to 4-quart saucepan, melt the butter over moderate heat. When the foam begins to subside, stir in ¾ cup of the flour and mix together thoroughly. Pour in the milk and, stirring constantly with a whisk, cook over high heat until the sauce comes to a boil and thickens heavily. Reduce the heat to low and simmer for 10 minutes, whisking frequently.

Remove the pan from the heat and, with a wooden spoon, vigorously beat in the egg yolks, one at a time. Add the salt and pepper and stir in the grated Gruyère and Emmentaler cheese. When thoroughly combined, pour the mixture into a lightly buttered 8-by-6-inch baking dish, spreading it out to a ½-inch thickness and smoothing the top with a spatula. Cool to room temperature, then cover with plastic wrap and refrigerate overnight, or for at least 8 hours, until firm.

With a pastry wheel or sharp knife, cut the cheese mixture into 2-inch squares, lifting them out of the dish with a small metal spatula and arranging them side by side on a strip of wax paper. One at a time, dip them into the remaining flour and, when they are completely coated on all sides, shake them free of any excess flour and dip them into the egg-and-milk mixture. Now coat them on all sides with the bread crumbs, patting them gently with the spatula to make them adhere. Arrange the squares on a large baking sheet and refrigerate for at least 1 hour, until the coating is firm.

Pour enough oil into a deep fryer or large, heavy saucepan to come 2 to 3 inches up the sides of the pan and heat the oil until it registers 375° on a deep-frying thermometer. Preheat the oven to its lowest setting. Line a large baking dish with a double thickness of paper towels and place it in the middle of the oven.

Deep-fry the *délices* 3 or 4 at a time, turning them with a slotted spoon for about 5 minutes, or until they are golden brown on both sides. As they brown, transfer them to the baking dish in the oven to keep them warm while you deep-fry the rest. Serve at once, as a first course or an accompaniment to drinks.

Raclette *(Switzerland)*
MELTED CHEESE WITH POTATOES AND PICKLES

To serve 4

½ pound imported Swiss *raclette*
   cheese, cut into 16 slices, each
   approximately ⅛ inch thick, 5
   inches long and 2 inches wide

4 freshly boiled small new potatoes,
   peeled and kept hot
4 to 8 small sour gherkins,
   preferably imported *cornichons*
4 to 8 pickled onions

Preheat the oven to 500° for at least 15 minutes. Heat four 10-inch oven-proof dinner plates in the oven for 3 to 5 minutes. To ensure the success of the *raclettes,* the plates must be very hot.

When ready to serve, remove the plates from the oven, grasping them with potholders, and, as quickly as you can, arrange four slices of the cheese in the center of each plate, overlapping them slightly. The cheese should begin to sizzle as soon as it comes in contact with the plate. At once, place the four plates on the floor of the oven (if you are using an electric oven, place the plates on a rack set in the first slot above the source of heat). In about 2 minutes (5 to 6 minutes in an electric oven) the cheese should melt to a creamy, bubbly mass; do not let it turn the slightest bit brown. Remove from the oven, place a potato and one or two gherkins and pickled onions on the side of each plate and serve at once, setting each plate on a service plate to prevent it from scorching the table.

NOTE: Swiss diners often consume at least 2 or 3 plates of *raclettes* in succession at one sitting. Should you want to do the same, double or triple all the ingredients and have two or three sets of dinner plates heating in the oven while the first batch of *raclettes* is being eaten.

Zwiebelwähe *(Switzerland)*
ONION-AND-CHEESE TART

To serve 6

PASTRY SHELL
1½ cups all-purpose flour
¼ teaspoon salt
6 tablespoons unsalted butter,
chilled and cut into ¼-inch bits
2 tablespoons lard or vegetable
   shortening, chilled and cut into
   ¼-inch bits
3 to 5 tablespoons ice water
1 tablespoon butter, softened

In a large chilled bowl, combine the flour, salt, chilled butter and the lard or vegetable shortening. With your fingertips rub the flour and fat together until they look like flakes of coarse meal. Be careful not to let the mixture become oily.

Pour 3 tablespoons of ice water over the mixture all at once, toss together lightly, and gather the dough into a ball. If the dough crumbles, add up to 2 tablespoons more ice water by drops until the particles adhere. Dust the pastry with a little flour and wrap it in wax paper. Refrigerate for at least 1 hour before using.

To prepare a baked but unfilled, or "blind," pastry shell, use a pastry brush to spread the tablespoon of softened butter over the bottom and sides of a 9-inch false-bottom fluted quiche pan, 1 inch deep.

On a lightly floured surface, pat the dough into a rough circle about 1 inch thick. Dust a little flour over and under it and roll it out, from the center to within an inch of the far edge of the pastry. Lift the dough and turn it clockwise about 2 inches; roll again from the center to within an inch or so of the far edge. Repeat—lifting, turning, rolling—until the circle is about ⅛ inch thick and 13 to 14 inches in diameter.

Drape the dough over the rolling pin, lift it up, and unroll it slackly over the quiche pan. Gently press it into the bottom and around the sides of the pan, being careful not to stretch the dough. Roll the pin over the rim of the pan, pressing down hard to trim off the excess dough.

Preheat the oven to 400°. Spread a sheet of buttered aluminum foil across the tin and press it gently against the bottom and sides to support the pastry as it bakes. Bake on the middle shelf of the oven for 10 minutes, then remove the foil. With a small knife prick the pastry where it has puffed up. Then return it to the oven for 10 minutes, or until it begins to brown. Remove it from the oven and cool.

FILLING

2 tablespoons vegetable oil
½ cup finely chopped onions
⅛ teaspoon paprika
¼ pound imported Swiss Gruyère
   cheese, coarsely grated (about 1 cup)
¼ pound imported Swiss
   Emmentaler cheese, coarsely
grated (about 1 cup)
2 eggs
½ cup light cream
½ cup milk
¼ teaspoon salt
⅛ teaspoon ground nutmeg,
   preferably freshly grated

To make the filling: Preheat the oven to 350°. In a heavy 6- to 8-inch skillet, heat the oil over moderate heat until a light haze forms above it. Add the onions and, stirring frequently, cook for about 5 minutes, or until they are soft and transparent but not brown. Stir in the paprika and set aside off the heat.

Place the Gruyère and Emmentaler cheese in a bowl and toss together until they are thoroughly combined.

Spread half of the cheese evenly in the baked pastry shell and scatter the onions over it. Then cover them with the remaining cheese. Beat the eggs, cream, milk, salt and nutmeg together with a wire whisk, and pour the mixture slowly and evenly over the cheese. Bake in the upper third of the oven for 10 minutes, then increase the heat to 425° and bake for 15 minutes longer, or until the filling has puffed and browned and a knife inserted in the center comes out clean.

To remove the tart from the pan, set it on a large jar or coffee can and slip down the outside rim. Run a long metal spatula under the pie to loosen the bottom, then slide the pie off onto a heated platter. Serve hot or at room temperature as a first or main course.

Ajja *(Tunisia)*
SCRAMBLED EGGS WITH HOT SAUSAGE AND PEPPERS

To serve 4

½ cup olive oil
1 pound highly seasoned sausage, such as Spanish *chorizos* or hot Italian sausage, cut into 1-inch rounds
1 teaspoon finely chopped garlic
1 teaspoon *hrisa (page 103)*
¼ teaspoon ground caraway seeds

3 medium-sized firm ripe tomatoes, peeled *(see bigos, page 80)* and quartered
½ cup cold water
Freshly ground black pepper
4 medium-sized green bell peppers, quartered, seeded, deribbed and cut lengthwise into ½-inch-wide strips
6 eggs

In a heavy 12-inch skillet, warm the oil over high heat until a light haze forms above it. Add the sausage, garlic, *hrisa* and caraway and, stirring frequently, cook until the sausage is lightly browned. Stir in the tomatoes, water and a liberal grinding of black pepper, and cook briskly until most of the liquid in the pan has evaporated and the tomatoes are reduced to a thick purée. Add the peppers and simmer partially covered for about 10 minutes. Do not let the peppers overcook; they should be somewhat firm to the bite.

Break the eggs into a bowl and, stirring constantly, pour them into the sausage mixture. Stirring with the flat of a table fork or a rubber spatula, cook over low heat until the eggs begin to form soft, creamy curds. Serve at once from a heated platter.

Banitsa *(Bulgaria)*
FLAKY CHEESE ROLLS

To make 16 rolls

½ pound unsalted butter, melted and cooled
1 pound *brynza* cheese, or substitute 1 pound *feta* cheese *(see Glossary)*

½ cup unflavored yoghurt
2 large eggs
16 sheets *filo* pastry, each about 16 to 18 inches long and 12 inches wide, thoroughly defrosted if frozen *(see Glossary)*

Preheat the oven to 400°. With a pastry brush, spread 2 tablespoons of the melted butter on 2 large baking sheets.

Crumble the cheese between your fingers, then force it through a food mill set over a deep bowl or rub it through a fine sieve with the back of a spoon. Add the yoghurt and eggs, and beat vigorously with a spoon until the mixture is smooth. Transfer about half of the cheese mixture to a pastry bag fitted with a ⅓-inch-wide plain tip.

Assemble each *banitsa* in the following fashion: Place one sheet of *filo* on a kitchen towel and brush it evenly with a teaspoon of the butter. Carefully fold the fragile pastry in half crosswise to make a two-layered rectangle about 12 inches long and 8 or 9 inches wide. Brush the top

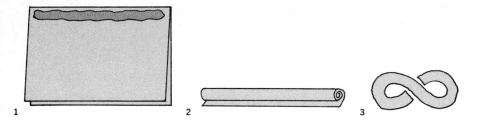

with about ½ teaspoon of the butter. Pipe a strand of the cheese mixture from the pastry bag along one long side of the rectangle, starting and ending ½ inch from the ends *(above, 1)*. Then roll the pastry into a narrow cylinder *(2)*, lifting the edge of the towel to help you, and brush it lightly but evenly with butter. Now gently curl one end around once or twice up to the middle of the cylinder, brushing it lightly with butter to keep it moist. Curl the other end around once or twice in the opposite direction, until you have created an S-shaped spiral *(3)*. With the aid of a long spatula, transfer the filled cheese roll to a baking sheet. Then proceed to make the remaining *banitsa* similarly, lining them up side by side on the baking sheets. Bake the *banitsa* in the middle of the oven for 20 minutes, or until they are crisp and a delicate golden brown. Slide them carefully onto a large heated platter and serve at once as a first course or as an accompaniment to drinks.

Brynza de Braila Frecata *(Romania)*
WHITE GOAT-CHEESE-AND-HERB SPREAD

To serve 6 to 8

½ pound *brynza* cheese, or substitute *feta* cheese *(see Glossary)*
½ pound unsalted butter, softened
2 tablespoons finely cut fresh chives
2 tablespoons finely cut fresh fennel leaves or ½ teaspoon powdered fennel
2 tablespoons finely chopped fresh parsley plus 8 fresh parsley sprigs
1 teaspoon imported paprika
1 teaspoon caraway seeds
2 medium-sized tomatoes, sliced
16 ripe black olives, preferably Mediterranean type
16 whole red radishes, trimmed, washed and dried
8 scallions, trimmed and cut into 3-inch lengths

Rub the cheese through a medium-meshed sieve into a bowl with the back of a spoon, or force the cheese through a food mill set over a bowl. Add the butter and beat vigorously with a wooden spoon, mashing the cheese and butter together against the sides of the bowl until the mixture is light and fluffy. Beat in the chives, fennel, chopped parsley, paprika and caraway seeds, and taste for seasoning.

Mound the cheese-and-herb mixture in the center of a platter and arrange the tomatoes, olives, parsley sprigs, radishes and scallions attractively around it. Serve at room temperature with rye or pumpernickel bread as a first course or as an accompaniment to cocktails.

Délicieuses Ostendaises *(Belgium)*
SHRIMP-AND-CHEESE FRITTERS

To make 32 fritters

½ pound raw medium-sized
   shrimp
5 tablespoons butter
10 tablespoons flour
2 cups milk
3 egg yolks
1½ teaspoons salt

½ teaspoon white pepper
1 cup finely grated Gruyère cheese
   (about ¼ pound)
2 eggs
4 teaspoons vegetable oil
2 cups dry fine bread crumbs
Vegetable oil for deep frying

Shell the shrimp. Devein them by making a shallow incision down their backs with a small, sharp knife and lifting out the black or white intestinal vein with the point of the knife Wash the shrimp under cold running water, pat them dry with paper towels, and slice them thin crosswise. Melt 1 tablespoon of the butter in a small skillet and, when the foam subsides, add the shrimp. Stirring constantly, cook over moderate heat for 2 to 3 minutes, or until the shrimp are firm and pink. With a slotted spoon, transfer the shrimp to a plate. Boil the liquid remaining in the uncovered skillet over high heat for a minute or two until it is reduced to a thick, syrupy glaze. Set it aside off the heat.

In a heavy 2- to 3-quart saucepan, melt the remaining 4 tablespoons of butter over moderate heat. When the foam begins to subside, stir in the flour and mix together thoroughly. Pour in the milk and, stirring constantly with a whisk, cook over high heat until the sauce comes to a boil and thickens heavily. Reduce the heat to low and simmer for 10 minutes, whisking frequently.

Remove the pan from the heat and, with a wooden spoon, vigorously beat in the egg yolks, one at a time. Add the salt and pepper, and stir in the shrimp, the shrimp glaze and the cheese. When the ingredients are thoroughly combined, pour the mixture into a lightly buttered 8-inch-square baking dish, spreading it out to all sides of the dish and smoothing the top with a spatula. Cool to room temperature, cover with plastic wrap and refrigerate for at least 6 hours, or until firm.

With a pastry wheel or sharp knife, cut the chilled shrimp mixture into 32 one-by-two-inch rectangles. Beat the eggs lightly with the oil and, one at a time, immerse the rectangles in the egg-and-oil mixture. Then dip both sides in the crumbs, patting them gently all over with the spatula to make the crumbs adhere. Arrange the rectangles on a large baking sheet and refrigerate for at least 1 hour, or until the coating is firm.

Pour oil into a deep fryer or large heavy saucepan to a depth of 2 to 3 inches and heat the oil until it reaches a temperature of 375° on a deep-frying thermometer. Preheat the oven to its lowest setting. Line a large baking dish with a double thickness of paper towels and place it on the middle shelf of the oven.

Deep-fry the *délicieuses* in the hot oil, 6 at a time, turning them occasionally with a slotted spoon, for 2 or 3 minutes, or until they are golden brown on all sides. As they brown, transfer them to the lined dish and keep them warm in the oven while you deep-fry the rest.

Arrange the *délicieuses ostendaises* attractively on a heated platter and serve them hot as a first course or as an accompaniment to drinks.

Purzheni Chushki s Sirene (Bulgaria)
FRIED PEPPERS STUFFED WITH CHEESE

To make 12 stuffed peppers

12 medium-sized Italian finger peppers (about 1½ pounds)	Freshly ground black pepper
	½ cup all-purpose flour
12 ounces *brynza* cheese, or substitute *feta* cheese (see Glossary)	3 cups soft fresh crumbs, made from homemade-type white bread, pulverized in a blender or finely shredded with a fork
6 ounces pot cheese	
2 eggs, plus 2 eggs lightly beaten	Vegetable oil for deep frying

Following the directions for peppers in oil *(page 86),* roast and peel the peppers. Cut out the stems and carefully scoop out the seeds, leaving the peppers intact.

Force the *brynza* or *feta* and the pot cheese through a food mill or rub them through a medium-meshed sieve into a bowl with the back of a spoon. Add 2 eggs and a few grindings of black pepper, and beat vigorously with a spoon until the mixture is smooth. Using a pastry bag fitted with a small plain tip, fill each of the roasted peppers with about 3 tablespoons of the cheese stuffing. One at a time, dip the peppers into the flour and shake gently to remove any excess. Turn the peppers about in the lightly beaten eggs and then roll them on all sides in the crumbs. If necessary, pat the crumbs into place with a small spatula to make them firmly adhere. Spread the peppers side by side on wax paper and refrigerate for about 30 minutes.

Pour the vegetable oil into a deep fryer or large heavy saucepan to a depth of at least 3 inches and heat the oil until it reaches a temperature of 375° on a deep-frying thermometer.

Fry the stuffed peppers in the hot oil, 3 or 4 at a time, turning them about with a slotted spoon for 2 to 3 minutes, or until they are richly and evenly browned. As they brown, transfer the peppers to paper towels to drain, then arrange them on a heated platter. Serve the peppers immediately, either whole as a first course or cut crosswise into 3 or 4 slices as a first course or an accompaniment to drinks.

Soups and Accompaniments

Boerenkaas Soep *(Netherlands)*
FARMERS CHEESE SOUP

To serve 4

4 tablespoons butter
1 cup finely chopped onions
2 medium-sized carrots, scraped and cut into ¼-inch dice
2 medium-sized boiling potatoes (about ½ pound), peeled and cut into ¼-inch dice
½ pound cauliflower, trimmed, washed and separated into small flowerets

¼ pound celery root (celeriac), peeled and cut into ¼-inch dice
1 quart chicken stock, fresh or canned
4 lean bacon slices
4 slices homemade-type white bread, cut about ½ inch thick and trimmed of all crusts
¼ pound imported Gouda cheese, cut into ⅛-inch slices

In a heavy 2- to 3-quart saucepan, melt the butter over moderate heat. Add the onions, carrots, potatoes, cauliflower and celery root. Stirring frequently, cook for about 5 minutes, then pour in the stock. Bring to a boil over high heat, partially cover the pan, and lower the heat. Simmer for 20 minutes, or until the vegetables are tender but not too soft.

Meanwhile, in a heavy 12-inch skillet, fry the bacon over moderate heat until the slices are brown and crisp around the edges and have rendered most of their fat. With tongs, transfer the bacon slices to paper towels to drain. Add the slices of bread to the fat remaining in the skillet and fry until they are crisp and brown on both sides. Set the fried bread aside on paper towels to drain.

Just before serving, preheat the broiler to its highest setting. Pour the soup into a 1½- to 2-quart ovenproof tureen or casserole. Float the bacon slices on top of the soup and cover each of them with a slice of fried bread and then a slice of cheese, arranging them so they mask the surface of the soup. Slide the tureen or casserole under the broiler (the top of the tureen should be about 3 inches from the heat) and broil for 2 or 3 minutes, until the cheese melts and turns a delicate brown.

Krupnik *(Poland)*

BARLEY VEGETABLE SOUP WITH SOUR CREAM

To serve 6 to 8

¼ ounce imported European dried mushrooms, preferably Polish dried mushrooms

2 cups boiling water

¼ pound chicken gizzards or hearts, cut into ¼-inch pieces

1 medium-sized carrot, scraped, cut lengthwise into quarters and sliced crosswise into ¼-inch lengths

¼ pound fresh green string beans, trimmed, washed and cut crosswise into ¼-inch lengths (about 1 cup)

¼ cup fresh green peas

2 quarts cold water

1 teaspoon unsalted butter

¼ cup pearl barley

3 medium-sized boiling potatoes (about ¾ pound), peeled, sliced crosswise into ½-inch rounds and then cut into ½-inch dice

Salt

Freshly ground black pepper

1 cup sour cream

2 tablespoons finely cut fresh dill leaves

Place the dried mushrooms in a small bowl, pour the boiling water over them, and soak for at least 2 hours, or until the mushrooms are soft and flexible. Drain the mushrooms (save the water) and chop them coarsely. In a heavy 3- to 4-quart casserole, combine the mushrooms and their soaking water, the chicken gizzards or hearts, the carrot, string beans and peas. Pour in the 2 quarts of cold water and bring to a boil over high heat. Reduce the heat to low and simmer partially covered for about 20 minutes, or until the chicken pieces are done and the vegetables are tender but still intact. Pour the contents of the casserole into a fine sieve set over a deep bowl, and set the chicken pieces and vegetables aside. Return the stock to the casserole.

Meanwhile, melt the teaspoon of butter over moderate heat. When the foam begins to subside, add the pearl barley and stir for 1 to 2 minutes, until the pearls glisten with butter. Do not let the barley brown.

Add the barley to the stock in the casserole and bring to a boil over high heat. Reduce the heat to low and simmer partially covered for 10 minutes. Add the potatoes and simmer partially covered for 20 minutes longer, or until the barley and potatoes are thoroughly cooked.

Return the chicken pieces and vegetables to the soup. Taste and season with salt and freshly ground pepper, then simmer for a few minutes to heat the chicken and vegetables through.

To serve, ladle the soup into a heated tureen or individual soup plates. Spoon the sour cream into a separate bowl or sauceboat, sprinkle the top with the dill, and serve with the soup.

Barszcz *(Poland)*
CLEAR BEET SOUP

To serve 8 to 10

BEEF STOCK

½ pound fresh beef brisket, in 1 piece
2 quarts cold water
2 thin slices lean bacon, cut into 1-inch pieces
1 medium-sized onion, peeled and quartered
1 medium-sized parsnip, peeled and coarsely chopped
1 medium-sized carrot, scraped and coarsely chopped
1 medium-sized garlic clove, peeled and coarsely chopped
½ small parsley root, peeled and coarsely chopped
1 small bay leaf
1 teaspoon salt
Freshly ground black pepper

Combine the beef brisket and 2 quarts of cold water in a heavy 4- to 5-quart enameled or stainless-steel casserole. Bring to a boil over high heat, meanwhile skimming off the foam and scum as they rise to the surface. Add the bacon, onion, parsnip, carrot, garlic, parsley root, bay leaf, 1 teaspoon salt and a few grindings of pepper. Then reduce the heat to low and simmer partially covered for about 2 hours, or until the brisket is tender and shows no resistance when pierced deeply with the point of a small skewer or knife.

With tongs or a slotted spoon, transfer the brisket to a plate and drape foil over it to keep it warm. Strain the contents of the casserole through a fine sieve into a deep bowl, pressing down hard on the bacon bits and vegetables with the back of a spoon to extract all their juices before discarding them. With a large spoon, skim off and discard as much of the surface fat as possible. Return the stock to the casserole.

BEET STOCK

2 pounds medium-sized firm young beets, peeled and coarsely grated
5 cups cold water
2 tablespoons red wine vinegar
1½ teaspoons salt
1 tablespoon strained fresh lemon juice
1 teaspoon sugar

In a 3- to 4-quart enameled or stainless-steel saucepan, bring the grated beets and 5 cups of cold water to a boil over high heat. Reduce the heat to moderate and cook uncovered for 10 minutes. Then reduce the heat to low, stir in the vinegar and 1 teaspoon of the salt, and simmer, partially covered, for 30 minutes. Strain the stock through a fine sieve into a glass or ceramic bowl, pressing down hard on the beets with the back of a spoon to extract all their juices before discarding them.

The beet and beef stocks may be set aside at this point if you wish to use the brisket to make *paszteciki (page 14),* pasties usually accompanying the soup. Just before serving, combine the stocks, add the remaining ½ teaspoon of salt, the lemon juice and sugar, and bring to a boil over high heat. Taste for seasoning and serve at once from a heated tureen or individual soup plates. If you have not prepared *paszteciki,* the brisket may be sliced and served with the soup.

Chłodnik (Poland)

COLD BEET SOUP WTH SHRIMP AND VEGETABLES

To serve 6 to 8

1 pound medium-sized firm young
   beets, peeled and coarsely grated
6½ cups cold water
3 tablespoons red wine vinegar
5 teaspoons salt
1½ teaspoons sugar
1 pound uncooked shrimp
1 cup sour cream
2 medium-sized cucumbers, peeled,
   sliced lengthwise in half, seeded
   and cut into ¼-inch dice
4 medium-sized scallions, including

2 inches of the green tops,
   trimmed, washed and cut
   crosswise into ¼-inch-thick
   rounds
4 red radishes, thinly sliced
4 tablespoons finely cut fresh dill
   leaves
3 tablespoons strained fresh lemon
   juice
A pinch of white pepper
1 lemon, thinly sliced (optional)
3 hard-cooked eggs, chilled and
   finely chopped (optional)

In a 3- to 4-quart enameled or stainless-steel saucepan, bring the grated beets and cold water to a boil over high heat. Reduce the heat to moderate and cook uncovered for 10 minutes. Then reduce the heat to low, stir in 2 tablespoons of the vinegar, 2 teaspoons of the salt and 1 teaspoon of the sugar, and simmer partially covered for 30 minutes. Drain the beets in a fine sieve set over a large bowl. Set the beets and the cooking liquid aside separately to cool to room temperature.

Peel the shrimp. Devein them by making a shallow incision down their backs with a small, sharp knife and lifting out the black or white intestinal vein with the point of the knife. Wash the shrimp under cold running water. Then bring 1 quart of water to a boil in a small pan, drop in the shrimp and cook briskly, uncovered, for about 3 minutes, or until they turn pink and are firm to the touch. Drain and coarsely chop the shrimp. Set aside to cool.

When the beet cooking liquid is completely cooled, beat in the sour cream with a wire whisk. Then stir in the beets, shrimp, cucumbers, scallions, radishes, 2 tablespoons of the dill, the lemon juice, the remaining tablespoon of vinegar, 3 teaspoons of salt and ½ teaspoon of sugar, and a pinch of white pepper. Taste for seasoning, cover the bowl tightly with plastic wrap, and refrigerate for at least 2 hours, or until the *chłodnik* is thoroughly chilled.

To serve, ladle the soup into a large chilled tureen or individual soup plates. Sprinkle the remaining dill on top and, if you like, garnish the *chłodnik* with thin slices of lemon and chopped hard-cooked eggs.

Paszteciki *(Poland)*
MEAT-FILLED PASTIES

To make 8 to 10 pasties

PASTRY

1 cup all-purpose flour	1 whole egg
⅛ teaspoon salt	5 tablespoons unsalted butter,
1 hard-cooked egg, yolk only	softened

Sift the flour and the ⅛ teaspoon of salt into a deep mixing bowl. With the back of a large spoon, rub the hard-cooked egg yolk through a fine sieve directly into the flour. Add the whole egg and stir until well combined, then beat in the softened butter, a tablespoon at a time. Transfer the dough to a lightly floured surface and knead it by pushing down on it with the heels of your hands, pressing it forward, and folding it back on itself. Knead until the dough is smooth and elastic, then wrap it in wax paper and refrigerate for at least 30 minutes, until it is firm.

FILLING

6 tablespoons unsalted butter	1-inch pieces
½ cup finely chopped onions	2 eggs, each lightly beaten in
½ pound cooked fresh beef	separate bowls
brisket *(see barszcz, page 12),*	1 teaspoon salt
trimmed of all fat and cut into	Freshly ground black pepper

Meanwhile, prepare the filling. In a heavy 8- to 10-inch skillet, melt 2 tablespoons of the butter over moderate heat. When the foam begins to subside, add the onions and, stirring frequently, cook for about 5 minutes, or until they art soft and transparent. Put the onions and beef through the finest blade of a meat grinder twice or, lacking a grinder, chop them as fine as possible.

Then, in the same skillet, melt the remaining 4 tablespoons of butter over moderate heat. Add the meat mixture and, stirring from time to time, cook over low heat until all the liquid in the pan has evaporated and the mixture is thick enough to hold its shape in a spoon. Remove the pan from the heat, let it cool to lukewarm, then stir in 1 beaten egg, the 1 teaspoon of salt and a few grindings of black pepper. Taste for seasoning, then transfer the filling to a bowl and set aside.

Preheat the oven to 350°. On a lightly floured surface, roll out the dough into a rectangle about 13 inches long, 8 inches wide and ⅛ inch thick. Spoon the filling lengthwise down the center of the rectangle and, with your hands, pat and shape the filling into a narrow cylinder about 11 inches long. Lightly brush the long sides of the rectangle of dough with cold water. Then fold one long edge over the cylinder, covering it completely, and turn the other long edge over the first. Brush the ends with cold water and fold them over the top, enclosing the filling.

Transfer the pastry, seam side down, to a large baking sheet and brush the top evenly with the remaining lightly beaten egg. Bake in the middle of the oven for 30 minutes, or until richly browned. Slide the *paszteciki* onto a heated platter, slice it diagonally into 1½-inch-wide pieces and serve as a first course or as an accompaniment to *barszcz (page 12)*.

Barszcz Wigilijny *(Poland)*
CHRISTMAS EVE BEET SOUP

To serve 4

MUSHROOM STOCK

3 ounces imported European dried mushrooms, preferably dried	Polish mushrooms
	4 cups boiling water

Place the mushrooms in a 2- to 3-quart enameled or stainless-steel saucepan and pour the boiling water over them. Let them soak at room temperature for at least 2 hours. Then place the pan over high heat and bring the soaking water to a boil. Lower the heat and simmer uncovered for about 2 hours, or until the liquid is reduced to ½ cup. Drain the stock through a fine sieve set over a bowl and set the mushrooms aside to be used, if you like, for *uszka,* the tiny dumplings usually served with this soup. Reserve the stock.

BEET STOCK

2½ pounds medium-sized firm young beets, peeled and coarsely grated	5 cups cold water
	2 tablespoons red wine vinegar
	2 teaspoons salt

Meanwhile, in a 3- to 4-quart enameled or stainless-steel saucepan, bring the grated beets and 5 cups of cold water to a boil over high heat. Reduce the heat to moderate and cook uncovered for 10 minutes. Then reduce the heat to low, stir in the vinegar and 2 teaspoons of salt, and simmer partially covered for 30 minutes. Strain the beet stock through a fine sieve into a bowl, pressing down hard on the beets with the back of a spoon to extract all their juice before discarding them.

½ teaspoon salt	1 tablespoon strained fresh lemon juice
¼ teaspoon sugar	

Return the beet stock to the saucepan in which it cooked, add the reserved mushroom stock, ½ teaspoon of salt, the sugar and lemon juice, and bring to a boil over high heat. Taste for seasoning and serve at once, accompanied, if you like, by *uszka (page 18)*.

Ciorba de Perisoare cu Carne *(Romania)*
TART SOUP WITH MEATBALLS

To serve 6 to 8

SOUP

1½ pounds pork bones, sawed into 1-inch pieces

1 veal shank bone, sawed into 1-inch pieces

2 quarts cold water

1 large onion, peeled

4 parsley sprigs plus 2 tablespoons finely chopped fresh parsley

3 large carrots, scraped and cut lengthwise into halves

2 medium-sized parsley roots, peeled and cut lengthwise into halves

1 medium-sized celery root (celeriac), peeled and cut lengthwise into halves

1 medium-sized firm ripe tomato, stemmed, peeled and coarsely chopped *(see bigos, page 80)*

4 cups sauerkraut juice

½ cup coarsely chopped leeks, including 2 inches of the green tops, thoroughly washed to rid them of all sand

½ cup coarsely chopped celery

2 tablespoons finely cut fresh fennel leaves, or substitute ½ teaspoon powdered fennel

½ teaspoon crumbled dried tarragon

1½ teaspoons salt

Combine the pork bones, veal bones and water in a heavy 6- to 8-quart casserole. Bring to a boil over high heat, meanwhile skimming off the foam and scum as they rise to the surface. Add the whole onion and parsley sprigs, partially cover the casserole, and simmer over low heat for 1 hour.

Then add the carrots, parsley roots, celery root and tomato, partially cover again and simmer for 45 minutes longer. With tongs or a slotted spoon, remove and discard the bones, onion and parsley sprigs. Stir in the sauerkraut juice, leeks, celery, the 2 tablespoons of chopped parsley, the fennel, tarragon and 1½ teaspoons of salt, and return the liquid to a boil. Lower the heat and simmer, partially covered, for 15 minutes.

MEATBALLS

¼ cup long-grain unconverted white rice

½ pound lean ground pork

½ pound lean ground veal

¼ cup finely chopped onions

1 tablespoon finely chopped fresh parsley

¼ teaspoon crumbled dried thyme

2 teaspoons salt

⅛ teaspoon freshly ground black pepper

1 egg, lightly beaten

Meanwhile, bring 1 quart of water to a boil in a saucepan. Stirring constantly, add the rice. Reduce the heat to moderate and cook uncovered for 10 minutes. Drain the rice in a sieve and run cold water over it to cool it.

In a deep bowl combine the ground pork, ground veal, partially cooked rice, onions, the 1 tablespoon of chopped parsley, thyme, the 2 teaspoons of salt and the black pepper. Knead vigorously with both hands, then add the lightly beaten egg and beat with a large spoon until the mixture is smooth and fluffy. Moistening your hands from time to time in cold water, shape the meat into compact balls each about 1 inch in diameter.

2 cups sour cream	1 tablespoon flour
2 egg yolks	1 tablespoon finely cut fresh dill leaves

When the soup has cooked its allotted time, add the meatballs. Cover the casserole tightly and simmer over low heat for 15 minutes. With a fork or whisk, beat 1 cup of the sour cream in a small bowl until smooth. Add the egg yolks, one at a time, and when they are completely absorbed, mix in the flour. Stir the mixture a few tablespoons at a time into the simmering soup and cook for 2 to 3 minutes longer, or until it thickens slightly. Do not let the *ciorba* come anywhere near a boil or it may curdle. Taste for seasoning and serve at once from a heated tureen or in individual soup plates. Combine the remaining cup of sour cream with the dill and serve separately in a bowl or sauceboat as a garnish to be added to the *ciorba* at the table.

Tarator (Bulgaria)
COLD CUCUMBER AND YOGHURT SOUP WITH WALNUTS

To serve 4

	⅓ cup walnuts, finely chopped
1 medium-sized or 2 small	1 tablespoon finely cut fresh dill
cucumbers	½ teaspoon finely chopped garlic
1½ teaspoons salt	2 tablespoons sunflower or olive oil
2 cups unflavored yoghurt	1 cup crushed ice cubes

With a small, sharp knife, peel the cucumber and slice it lengthwise into halves. Scoop out and discard the seeds by running the tip of a teaspoon gently down the center of each half. Cut the cucumber halves into ¼-inch dice, place in a small bowl, and sprinkle evenly with ½ teaspoon of salt. Set aside at room temperature for about 15 minutes. Then transfer the cucumber dice to a sieve, wash briefly under cold running water, and let them drain. Spread the cucumbers out on paper towels and pat them thoroughly dry.

Combine the diced cucumbers, unflavored yoghurt, chopped walnuts, dill, garlic and the remaining teaspoon of salt in a deep bowl, tossing them about with a spoon until they are thoroughly mixed. Stir in the sunflower or olive oil by the teaspoonful, making sure each addition is well absorbed before adding more.

Ladle the soup into 4 individual bowls or soup plates, dividing it evenly among them, and refrigerate the soup for at least 1 hour, or until thoroughly chilled. Drop about ¼ cup of crushed ice cubes into each bowl immediately before serving.

Uszka

TINY DUMPLINGS FILLED WITH MUSHROOMS ("LITTLE EARS")

To make about 5 dozen dumplings

STUFFING

6 tablespoons butter	shredded with a fork
½ cup finely chopped onions	3 ounces dried mushrooms, cooked
1 tablespoon soft fresh crumbs	and cooled (see barszcz
made from homemade-type white	Wigilijny, page 15)
bread, trimmed of crusts and	1 egg white
pulverized in a blender or finely	1 teaspoon salt

In a heavy 6- to 8-inch skillet, melt 2 tablespoons of the butter over moderate heat. When the foam begins to subside, add the onions and, stirring frequently, cook for about 5 minutes, or until they are soft and translucent but not brown. Stir in the bread crumbs and, when they glisten with butter, remove the pan from the heat and mix in the mushrooms. Then put the mixture twice through the finest blade of a food grinder.

Melt the remaining 4 tablespoons of butter in the same skillet. Add the ground mushroom mixture and, stirring from time to time, cook over low heat until most of the liquid in the pan has evaporated. Remove the skillet from the heat and stir the egg white and 1 teaspoon of salt into the mushroom stuffing. Taste for seasoning and cool to room temperature.

DOUGH

1 whole egg plus 1 egg white	2¼ teaspoons salt
1 tablespoon cold water	1 cup all-purpose flour

Meanwhile, prepare the dough in the following fashion: In a deep bowl, beat the egg, egg white, water and ¼ teaspoon of the salt together with a spoon until they are smooth. Beating constantly, sift in the flour a few tablespoons at a time. Continue to beat, or knead with your hands, until the dough can be gathered into a compact ball.

On a lightly floured surface, roll the dough into a paper-thin rectangle about 15 inches long and 9 inches wide. Turn the dough at right angles after each rolling and sprinkle flour over and under it to prevent it from sticking to the board. Then with a pastry wheel or sharp knife cut the dough into sixty 1½-inch squares. Cover them with a dampened kitchen towel to keep them moist while you fill and shape the dumplings.

To make each *uszka*, place about ¼ teaspoon of the mushroom filling in the center of a square of dough (*opposite, 1*). With a finger dipped in cold water, moisten the edges. Fold the square in half diagonally to create a triangle (2) and press the edges securely together. Then lift up the two points of the base and pinch them together (3). As the dumplings are shaped, cover them with a dampened towel and set aside.

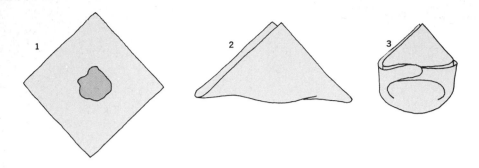

In a heavy 3- to 4-quart casserole, bring 2 quarts of water and 2 teaspoons of salt to a boil over high heat. Stirring gently with a wooden spoon, drop in the dumplings, a large handful at a time. Reduce the heat to low and simmer each batch for 5 minutes, or until the dumplings are tender to the bite. With a slotted spoon, transfer them to a bowl and drape foil over them to keep them warm.

As soon as all of the dumplings are cooked, arrange them in individual soup plates and ladle a hot clear soup such as *barszcz Wigilijny* (*page 15*) over them. Although the Poles often serve as many as 12 *uszka* per bowl, you may prefer to serve somewhat fewer and reserve the rest (covered with plastic wrap and refrigerated) for future use. They will keep in this fashion for up to a week. Or you may freeze some of the uncooked dumplings; in that case, defrost them thoroughly before cooking.

Gerstensuppe (Switzerland)
BARLEY SOUP

To serve 6 to 8

½ cup pearl barley
1 pound smoked ham hocks
1 teaspoon salt
Freshly ground black pepper
2½ quarts cold water

1 cup finely chopped leeks including
    2 inches of the green tops
½ cup finely chopped celery
½ cup finely chopped onions
1 medium-sized baking potato,
    peeled and finely chopped
1 cup heavy cream

Combine the barley, ham hocks, salt, a few grindings of black pepper and the water in a heavy 4- to 6-quart casserole and bring to a boil over high heat. Reduce the heat to low, cover the pan partially, and simmer for 45 minutes. Add the leeks, celery, onions and potato, and continue to simmer for 30 minutes longer, or until the barley is soft and the vegetables tender. Remove and discard the ham hocks and, stirring constantly, pour in the cream in a slow stream. Simmer for 2 or 3 minutes to heat the soup thoroughly, then taste for seasoning and serve at once from a heated tureen or in individual soup plates.

Soupe à l'Ardennaise *(Belgium)*
CREAM OF ENDIVE SOUP

To serve 6 to 8

4 tablespoons butter
6 medium-sized Belgian endives
    (about 1 pound), trimmed,
    washed and finely chopped
2 medium-sized leeks, including 2
    inches of the green tops,
    trimmed, thoroughly washed to
    rid them of all sand, then finely

    chopped
1 medium-sized baking potato
    (about ½ pound), peeled and
    finely chopped
1 tablespoon salt
¼ teaspoon white pepper
6 cups milk
4 tablespoons butter, softened

In a heavy 3- to 4-quart casserole, melt 4 tablespoons of butter over moderate heat. When the foam begins to subside, add the endives and leeks, and stir until they are evenly coated with the butter. Reduce the heat to low, cover tightly, and cook for about 10 minutes, or until the vegetables are soft and translucent but not brown. Stir in the potato, salt and pepper, pour in the milk, and bring to a simmer over moderate heat, stirring from time to time. Reduce the heat to low again and simmer uncovered for about 45 minutes. When the soup is finished the potatoes will have dissolved almost completely to create a light purée.

    Taste for seasoning, swirl the softened butter into the soup, and serve at once from a heated tureen or in individual soup plates.

Erwtensoep *(Netherlands)*
GREEN PEA SOUP

To serve 8 to 10

2 cups dried green split peas (1
    pound), thoroughly washed
2 large fresh meaty pig's feet
½ pound mildly cured salt pork in
    1 piece with rind removed
4 quarts water
4 medium-sized boiling potatoes
    (about 1½ pounds), peeled and
    cut into ¼-inch dice
4 medium-sized leeks, including 2
    inches of the green tops,
    trimmed, washed to remove any

    sand, and finely chopped
1 medium-sized celery root
    (celeriac), peeled and cut into
    ¼-inch dice
¼ cup finely chopped fresh celery
    leaves
½ pound precooked smoked
    sausage, such as *kielbasa,* sliced
    into ¼-inch-thick rounds
¼ teaspoon crumbled dried
    summer savory
Freshly ground black pepper

In a heavy 6- to 8-quart casserole combine the split peas, pig's feet, salt pork and water. Bring to a boil over high heat, skimming off the foam and scum as they rise to the surface. Reduce the heat to low, partially cover the pan, and simmer for 3 hours. Then add the potatoes, leeks, celery root and celery leaves, and simmer, partially covered, for 30 minutes.

With tongs or a slotted spoon, transfer the pig's feet and salt pork to a cutting board. Remove and discard the skin, gristle and bones from the pig's feet, then cut the meat and the salt pork into ½-inch dice.

Return the diced meats to the soup and add the sliced sausage, crumbled summer savory and a few grindings of black pepper. Stirring constantly, bring the soup to a simmer over moderate heat and cook for a few minutes to heat the sausage through.

Taste for seasoning and serve at once from a heated tureen or in individual soup plates.

Harira *(Morocco)*
RAMADAN SOUP WITH LAMB

To serve 4

2 tablespoons olive oil
½ pound lean boneless lamb shoulder, trimmed of excess fat, sliced ⅛ inch thick and cut into strips 1 inch long and ⅛ inch wide
½ teaspoon ground ginger
¼ teaspoon turmeric
2 medium-sized firm ripe tomatoes, peeled, seeded and cut into 1-inch chunks *(see bigos, page 80)*

½ cup finely chopped onions
2 tablespoons finely chopped fresh coriander *(cilantro)*
1½ teaspoons salt
1½ teaspoons freshly ground black pepper
1 quart cold water
¼ cup *orzo (see Glossary)*
2 eggs, lightly beaten
2 teaspoons strained fresh lemon juice
Ground cinnamon

In a heavy 3- to 4-quart casserole, warm the oil over high heat until a light haze forms above it. Brown the lamb in the hot oil, turning the strips about frequently with a slotted spoon and regulating the heat so they color richly and evenly without burning. Stir in the ginger and turmeric, then add the tomatoes, onions, coriander, salt, pepper and water. Bring to a boil over high heat, reduce the heat to low, and simmer partially covered for 45 minutes.

Raise the heat to high and, when the soup comes to a boil, stir in the *orzo*. Stirring from time to time, cook uncovered over moderate heat for about 10 minutes, until the *orzo* is tender. Then remove the casserole from the heat and beat in the eggs, lemon juice and a sprinkling of cinnamon. Taste for seasoning and serve at once.

NOTE: When the eggs are added to the soup, they will separate into strands. Do not be concerned; this is a characteristic of *harira*.

The recipes for fish soup (below) and chicken in lemon cream soup (opposite) have more in common than they appear to. Both Flemish, they are called "waterzooï": "water on the boil." All versions of "waterzooï" are prepared with a vegetable base (although the vegetables may vary) and with a broth that is thickened somewhat before serving. Finally, "waterzooï" is splendidly practical, comprising both a soup and main course.

Waterzooi de Poissons (Belgium)
FLEMISH FISH SOUP

To serve 6

3 pounds fish trimmings: heads, tails and bones from any white-fleshed fish
1 large onion, peeled and thinly sliced
8 sprigs fresh parsley
1 large bay leaf
½ teaspoon whole black peppercorns
2 cups dry white wine
3 quarts cold water
2 tablespoons butter

1 cup finely chopped celery
1 pound eel, cleaned, skinned and cut crosswise into 2-inch lengths
1 pound perch, cleaned, trimmed and cut into ½-inch-thick pieces
1 pound pike, cleaned, trimmed and cut into ½-inch-thick pieces
1 pound carp, cleaned, trimmed and cut into ½-inch-thick pieces
6 tablespoons butter, cut into ¼-inch bits
¼ teaspoon crumbled dried thyme
Salt

Combine the fish trimmings, onions, parsley sprigs, bay leaf and peppercorns in a 6- to 8-quart enameled or stainless-steel pot. Pour in the wine and water and, stirring occasionally, bring to a boil over high heat.

Reduce the heat to low and simmer, partially covered, for 30 minutes. Then strain the stock through a fine sieve set over a deep bowl or saucepan, pressing down hard on the fish trimmings and vegetables with the back of a spoon before discarding them.

In a heavy 4- to 5-quart enameled or stainless-steel casserole, melt the 2 tablespoons of butter over moderate heat. When the foam subsides, stir in the celery. Cover tightly and reduce the heat to low. Simmer 5 minutes.

When the celery is soft but not brown, spread the pieces of eel, perch, pike and carp evenly on top, and dot the fish with the bits of butter. Pour in 6 cups of the strained fish stock and add the crumbled thyme. Bring to a simmer over high heat, then reduce the heat to low and cover the casserole tightly. Simmer for 6 to 8 minutes, or until the flesh flakes easily when it is prodded gently with a fork. Do not overcook the fish.

With a slotted spoon or spatula transfer the pieces of fish to a heated tureen. Bring the stock remaining in the casserole to a boil over high heat and cook briskly, uncovered, for 6 to 8 minutes, or until it reaches the intensity of flavor you like. Taste the stock for seasoning, pour it over the fish in the tureen and serve at once.

Waterzooi à la Gantoise (Belgium)

FLEMISH CHICKEN IN LEMON CREAM SOUP

To serve 8 to 10

A 5-pound stewing fowl, cut into 8
   pieces
The fowl giblets
1 pound lean beef chuck or shin
1 veal shank, sawed into 1-inch
   pieces
4 quarts water
3 cups coarsely chopped onions
3 medium-sized celery stalks,
   trimmed and coarsely chopped

2 medium-sized leeks, white part
   only, trimmed, thoroughly
   washed to remove any sand, and
   coarsely chopped
2 medium-sized carrots, scraped and
   coarsely chopped
2 teaspoons salt
4 egg yolks
1 cup heavy cream
1 to 2 tablespoons strained fresh
   lemon juice
⅛ teaspoon white pepper

Combine the fowl, giblets, beef, veal shank and water in a heavy 8- to 10-quart pot. Bring to a boil over high heat, skimming off the scum and foam as they rise to the surface. Add the onions, celery, leeks, carrots and salt, then reduce the heat to low and simmer partially covered for about 2½ hours. When the bird is tender, lift the pieces out of the stock with tongs and place them on a plate. Discard the veal bones and giblets and set the beef aside for another use. With a small knife, remove and discard the skin and bones from the fowl and cut the meat into strips about 2 inches long and 1 inch wide.

Strain the entire contents of the pot through a fine sieve set over a heavy 5- to 6-quart casserole, pressing down hard on the vegetables with the back of a spoon before discarding them. Let the liquid rest for a few minutes, then with a large spoon skim off and discard as much fat as possible from the surface.

Boil briskly, uncovered, over high heat until the soup has cooked down to about 10 cups, then reduce the heat to low. When the soup is barely simmering, beat the egg yolks and cream together with a whisk or fork and pour it into the soup in a thin stream, stirring all the while. Add the strips of chicken and continue to stir until the *waterzooi* thickens slightly and the chicken is heated through. Do not allow the soup to come anywhere near a boil or it will curdle. Add 1 tablespoon of the lemon juice and the white pepper, taste for seasoning, and add the remaining lemon juice if you prefer the soup somewhat tart. Serve at once from a heated tureen or in deep individual soup plates.

Ciorba de Peste *(Romania)*
FISH SOUP WITH GARLIC SAUCE

To serve 4 to 6

STOCK
1 pound fish trimmings: the heads,
   tails and bones of any firm white-
   fleshed fish

1½ cups coarsely chopped onions
1 medium-sized bay leaf
1 teaspoon salt
6 cups cold water

Combine the fish trimmings, chopped onions, bay leaf, 1 teaspoon of salt and the 6 cups of water in a heavy 3- to 4-quart enameled or stainless-steel casserole. Bring to a boil over high heat, reduce the heat to low, and simmer partially covered for 30 minutes. Strain the entire contents of the casserole through a fine sieve into a deep bowl, pressing down hard on the fish trimmings and onions with the back of a spoon to extract all their juices before discarding them.

FISH SOUP
½ pound boned skinless halibut or
   other firm white-fleshed fish,
   coarsely chopped
1 teaspoon salt
¼ teaspoon freshly ground black
   pepper
2 pounds halibut or other firm
   white-fleshed fish steaks, each cut

   1 inch thick
1 tablespoon finely chopped garlic
   mashed to a smooth paste with
   ½ teaspoon salt
1 medium-sized cucumber, peeled,
   seeded and cut into ¼-inch dice
2 tablespoons distilled white
   vinegar

Pour the stock back into the casserole and add the chopped fish. Stirring occasionally, bring to a boil over high heat. Reduce the heat to its lowest point and simmer uncovered for about 15 minutes, or until the fish can be easily mashed with the back of a spoon. Purée the contents of the casserole in a food mill, or rub them through a coarse sieve, and return to the casserole. Stir in the 1 teaspoon of salt and ¼ teaspoon of pepper, and immerse the fish steaks in the soup. Bring to a simmer over moderate heat and poach partially covered for 5 to 8 minutes, or until the fish flakes easily when prodded gently with a fork. Do not overcook.

With a slotted spatula, transfer the steaks to a large heated tureen or individual soup plates. With a whisk, beat 1 cup of the soup into the garlic paste and pour the mixture into a sauceboat. Add the cucumber and vinegar to the remaining soup, taste for seasoning, and ladle over the fish steaks. Serve at once, accompanied by the garlic sauce.

Busecca *(Switzerland)*
TRIPE, WHITE BEAN AND VEGETABLE SOUP

To serve 8

1 pound tripe, cut into 1½-by-⅛-inch strips
1½ cups dried white navy or pea beans
½ cup olive oil
1 cup coarsely chopped onions
1 cup coarsely chopped scraped carrots
1 cup coarsely chopped celery
1 cup coarsely chopped leeks, including 2 inches of the green tops
1 cup coarsely chopped cabbage
4 medium-sized firm ripe tomatoes,
peeled, seeded and coarsely chopped *(see bigos, page 80)*
4 medium-sized garlic cloves, peeled and coarsely chopped
1 teaspoon crumbled dried oregano
1 tablespoon salt
¼ teaspoon freshly ground black pepper
1 quart chicken stock, fresh or canned
1 cup coarsely chopped fresh spinach
2 medium-sized boiling potatoes, peeled and cut into ½-inch dice
2 tablespoons tomato paste

Place the tripe in a large saucepan and add enough cold water to cover it by at least 2 inches. Bring to a boil over high heat, then reduce the heat to low and simmer partially covered for 1½ hours. Drain the tripe in a sieve or colander and set aside.

Meanwhile, combine the beans and 3 quarts of water in a heavy saucepan and bring to a boil over high heat. Boil briskly for 2 minutes, remove the pan from the heat, and let the beans soak for 1 hour. Pour off the soaking water and set the beans aside.

In a heavy 6- to 8-quart casserole, heat the oil over moderate heat until a light haze forms above it. Add the onions, carrots, celery, leeks and cabbage. Stir well, cover the casserole, and simmer over low heat for 15 minutes, or until the vegetables are soft but not brown. Add the tripe, beans, tomatoes, garlic, oregano, salt, pepper and chicken stock and, stirring frequently, bring to a boil over high heat. Reduce the heat to low and simmer partially covered for 1 hour. Then stir in the spinach, potatoes and tomato paste, and continue to simmer for about 20 minutes longer, or until the beans and potatoes are tender but not falling apart. Taste for seasoning and serve at once from a heated tureen or soup plates.

Fish and Shellfish

Karp po Zydowsku (Poland)
SWEET-AND-SOUR JEWISH-STYLE CARP

To serve 6 to 8

1 pound fish trimmings: the head, tail and bones of any firm white-fleshed fish
2 quarts cold water
3 cups coarsely chopped onions
1 large bay leaf, crumbled
1 teaspoon plus 2 tablespoons salt
12 whole black peppercorns
½ cup distilled white vinegar

½ cup sugar
½ cup seedless raisins
¼ cup halved blanched almonds
5 teaspoons citric (sour) salt *(see Glossary)*
A 3- to 3½-pound carp, cleaned and cut into ½-inch-thick steaks, or substitute 3 to 3½ pounds salmon steaks, cut ½ inch thick
1 lemon, thinly sliced

Combine the fish trimmings and water in a 4- to 5-quart enameled or stainless-steel casserole. Bring to a boil over high heat, meanwhile skimming off all the foam and scum that rise to the surface. Add the onions, bay leaf, 1 teaspoon of the salt and the peppercorns, reduce the heat to low, and simmer partially covered for 30 minutes. Strain this fish stock through a fine sieve into a deep bowl, pressing down hard on the fish trimmings and onions with the back of a spoon to extract all their juices before discarding them.

Return the strained stock to the casserole and stir in the vinegar, sugar, raisins, almonds, citric salt and the remaining 2 tablespoons of salt. Bring to a boil over high heat, stirring until the sugar and salt dissolve. Cook briskly for 3 to 4 minutes, reduce the heat to low and add the fish steaks. Cover the casserole partially and simmer gently, undisturbed, for 8 to 10 minutes, or until the flesh flakes easily when the fish is prodded gently with a fork.

With a slotted spatula, transfer the fish to an enameled or glass baking dish at least 2 inches deep and large enough to hold the steaks in one layer. Arrange the slices of lemon over the fish and pour the entire contents of the casserole into the dish. Cool to room temperature, then cover tightly with plastic wrap and refrigerate until the sauce has jelled. Serve cold, as a first course or light luncheon dish.

Anguilles au Vert *(Belgium)*
EELS IN GREEN SAUCE

To serve 4 to 6

6 tablespoons butter
1 cup coarsely chopped fresh
spinach leaves (the leaves
stripped from about ¼ pound
fresh spinach and the stems
discarded)
½ cup coarsely chopped fresh
parsley, preferably flat-leaf Italian-
type parsley
4 tablespoons coarsely chopped
fresh sorrel, or substitute 2
tablespoons bottled or canned
sorrel, strained, then squeezed
dry in a towel
¼ cup finely cut fresh chervil, or
substitute 2 tablespoons crumbled
dried chervil
1 tablespoon finely cut fresh mint,

or substitute 2 teaspoons
crumbled dried mint (optional)
1 teaspoon finely cut fresh thyme,
or substitute ½ teaspoon
crumbled dried thyme
1 teaspoon finely cut fresh tarragon,
or substitute ½ teaspoon
crumbled dried tarragon
½ teaspoon finely cut fresh sage,
or substitute ¼ teaspoon
crumbled dried leaf sage
2 pounds eels, cleaned, skinned and
cut crosswise into 2-inch lengths
1 cup dry white wine
1½ teaspoons salt
Freshly ground black pepper
2 egg yolks
2 tablespoons strained fresh lemon
juice

In a heavy 12-inch skillet, melt the butter over moderate heat. When the foam begins to subside, add the spinach, parsley, sorrel, chervil, mint, thyme, tarragon and sage. Stirring frequently, cook uncovered for 2 to 3 minutes, until the greens begin to wilt.

Add the eels and, turning the slices frequently, cook over moderate heat for 5 minutes, but do not let them brown. Then stir in the wine, salt and a few grindings of pepper, cover tightly, and simmer over low heat for 15 minutes, or until the eel shows no resistance when pierced with the tip of a knife.

In a small bowl, beat the egg yolks with a fork only long enough to combine them. Stir in ½ cup of the simmering cooking liquid and mix well, then slowly pour the mixture into the skillet, stirring gently all the while. Add the lemon juice and taste for seasoning.

Transfer the entire contents of the skillet to a shallow glass or enameled baking dish. Cool to room temperature, then cover with plastic wrap and refrigerate for at least 4 hours, or until thoroughly chilled. Serve cold, as a first course.

NOTE: If you prefer, you may serve the *anguilles au vert* hot, the moment they are done, as many Belgians do.

Gratin d'Huîtres d'Ostende *(Belgium)*
CREAMED OYSTERS AND SHRIMP IN SHELLS

To serve 4

½ pound medium-sized raw
   shrimp (16 to 20 per pound)
6 tablespoons butter
2 dozen fresh oysters, shucked, with
   the deeper half shell of each
   oyster and all the oyster liquor
   reserved
½ to 1 cup milk
2 tablespoons dry white wine
3 tablespoons all-purpose flour

1 egg yolk
¼ teaspoon white pepper
1 teaspoon salt
Rock salt or coarse salt (optional;
   see note page 33)
¼ cup soft fresh crumbs made
   from homemade-type white
   bread, pulverized in a blender or
   finely shredded with a fork
½ cup freshly grated imported
   Gruyère or Emmentaler cheese

Preheat the oven to 450°. Shell the shrimp. Devein them by making a shallow incision down their backs with a small, sharp knife and lifting out the black or white intestinal vein with the point of the knife. Wash the shrimp under cold running water and pat them dry with paper towels, then chop them coarsely. Melt 2 tablespoons of the butter in a small skillet. When the foam begins to subside, drop in the shrimp and, stirring constantly, cook over moderate heat for 2 or 3 minutes, until they begin to turn pink. Set aside off the heat.

Pour the oyster liquor into a large measuring cup and add enough milk to make 1¾ cups. Stir in the wine. In a heavy 8- to 10-inch skillet, melt the 4 remaining tablespoons of butter over moderate heat, but do not let it brown. Then stir in the flour and mix together thoroughly. Pour in the milk, oyster liquor and wine mixture and, stirring constantly with a whisk, cook over high heat until the sauce boils and thickens lightly. Reduce the heat to low and simmer for about 3 minutes. Then beat the egg yolk lightly in a bowl, add about ¼ cup of the sauce, and whisk the egg-yolk mixture into the sauce in the pan. Add the pepper and salt and taste for seasoning. Remove the pan from the heat and stir in the reserved shrimp.

Fill a large shallow baking dish to a depth of about ¼ inch with rock salt or coarse salt. (The salt will not only act as a bed for the oysters but also help keep them hot after they are cooked.) Spoon about 1 tablespoon of the shrimp sauce into each oyster shell, top with an oyster, and blanket the oyster with a second tablespoon of the shrimp sauce. Arrange the filled shells side by side in the salt-lined baking dish. Bake in the top third of the oven for about 8 minutes, or until the sauce has barely begun to bubble. Sprinkle the oysters evenly with the bread crumbs and the cheese. Return them to the oven for another 3 or 4 minutes, or until the cheese melts and the crumbs brown lightly. You may then, if you like, slide them under the broiler (about 3 inches from the heat) for a minute or two to brown the tops further. Serve at once.

Truite à la Crème Zugoise *(Switzerland)*
TROUT IN HERBED CREAM SAUCE

To serve 4

4 tablespoons butter
3 tablespoons finely chopped shallots, or substitute 3 tablespoons finely chopped scallions, white parts only
1 teaspoon finely chopped fresh parsley
1 teaspoon crumbled dried chervil

1 teaspoon crumbled dried thyme
1 teaspoon crumbled dried tarragon
1½ cups Neuchâtel or other dry white wine
8 four-ounce trout fillets with the skins left on
1 teaspoon salt
⅛ teaspoon white pepper
2 cups heavy cream

In a heavy 12-inch skillet, melt the butter over moderate heat. When the foam begins to subside, add the shallots (or scallions) and, stirring frequently, cook for about 5 minutes, or until they are soft and transparent but not brown. Watch carefully for any sign of burning and regulate the heat accordingly. Stir in the parsley, chervil, thyme and tarragon, then pour in the wine and mix well. Remove the skillet from the heat.

Pat the trout fillets completely dry with paper towels and sprinkle them on both sides with the salt and pepper. Arrange them on top of the herbs in the skillet in one layer, overlapping them slightly if necessary. Cut a circle of foil 12 or 13 inches in diameter and press it gently but firmly over the fish.

Return the skillet to moderate heat and simmer the trout for about 5 minutes, or until the flesh flakes easily when prodded gently with a fork. With a slotted spatula, transfer the fillets to a heated platter and drape fresh foil over it to keep the fish warm while you prepare the sauce.

Stirring constantly with a wire whisk or large spoon, bring the liquid remaining in the skillet to a boil over high heat and cook briskly until it is reduced to a thin film that barely covers the bottom of the pan. Reduce the heat to moderate and, still stirring, pour in the cream and any liquid that has accumulated around the fish. Continue to boil the sauce, stirring occasionally, until it is thick enough to coat the whisk heavily. This may take from 5 to 10 minutes. Taste for seasoning, then pour the sauce over the trout, masking them completely. Serve at once. Traditionally, the trout are accompanied by a separate bowl of freshly boiled new potatoes.

Poissons à l'Escavêche *(Belgium)*

PICKLED FISH

To serve 6 to 8

1 pound perch, cut into pieces 2 inches thick
1 pound pike, cut into pieces 2 inches thick
1 pound carp, cut into pieces 2 inches thick
1 pound eel, cleaned, skinned and cut into 2-inch lengths
1 teaspoon plus 1 tablespoon salt
Freshly ground black pepper
⅓ cup plus 4 tablespoons flour
9 tablespoons butter

3 medium-sized onions (about 1 pound), peeled, cut crosswise into ⅛-inch-thick slices and separated into rings
2 medium-sized lemons, peeled and cut crosswise into ⅛-inch-thick slices
2 cups dry white wine
2 cups water
1 cup white wine vinegar
1 teaspoon crumbled dried tarragon
10 whole peppercorns

Pat the pieces of perch, pike, carp and eel completely dry with paper towels. Sprinkle the fish on all sides with 1 teaspoon of the salt and a few grindings of black pepper. Dip each piece in the ⅓ cup of flour and, when it is evenly coated, shake vigorously to remove any excess.

In a heavy 10- to 12-inch skillet, melt 6 tablespoons of the butter over moderate heat. When the foam begins to subside, fry the fish a few pieces at a time until they are golden brown on both sides. As they brown, transfer the fish to paper towels to drain. With a small knife, remove the skin and bones from the perch, pike and carp. Then arrange the fish, including the eel, in one layer in an enameled or glass casserole at least 2 inches deep and large enough to hold them comfortably. Spread the onions and lemons over the fish and set aside.

Meanwhile, in a 2- to 3-quart enameled or stainless-steel saucepan, melt the remaining 3 tablespoons of butter over moderate heat. Stir in the remaining 4 tablespoons of flour and mix together thoroughly. Pour in the wine, water and vinegar, and stirring constantly with a whisk, cook over high heat until the sauce comes to a boil and thickens lightly. Add the tarragon, peppercorns and the remaining tablespoon of salt, reduce the heat to low, and simmer for about 5 minutes to remove any raw taste of the flour.

Pour the sauce over the fish and cool to room temperature. Cover tightly with foil or plastic wrap and refrigerate for at least 2 days before serving as a light luncheon dish or first course.

Sharan Polnen s Orechki (Bulgaria)
BAKED CARP STUFFED WITH RICE AND NUTS

To serve 6

½ pound filberts or hazelnuts
2 tablespoons unconverted long-
grain white rice
A 3- to 3½-pound carp, cleaned
but with head and tail left on
1½ teaspoons salt

6 tablespoons olive oil
½ cup finely chopped onions
⅛ teaspoon ground hot red pepper
(cayenne)
Freshly ground black pepper
¼ cup strained fresh lemon juice
combined with ½ cup water

Drop the filberts or hazelnuts into enough boiling water to cover them completely and boil briskly for 2 minutes. Drain the nuts in a sieve and, with a small, sharp knife, peel them while they are still hot. Grind the nuts in an electric blender or with a nut grinder or pulverize them with a mortar and pestle.

In a 2- to 3-quart saucepan, bring 1 quart of lightly salted water to a boil over high heat. Add the rice and boil briskly, uncovered, for 10 minutes, or until partially cooked. Drain the rice in a sieve or colander, run cold water over it, and set it aside.

Preheat the oven to 400°. Wash the carp under cold running water and pat it completely dry with paper towels. Sprinkle the fish, inside and out, with 1 teaspoon of the salt.

Heat 2 tablespoons of the olive oil in a heavy 8- to 10-inch skillet. When a light haze forms above it, add the onions and, stirring frequently, cook over moderate heat until they are soft and translucent but not brown. Add the nuts, rice, red pepper, the remaining ½ teaspoon of salt and a few grindings of pepper, and stir for 2 to 3 minutes. Cool to lukewarm, then spoon the mixture into the fish and close the opening with small skewers and kitchen string or sew it up with heavy thread.

Pour the remaining 3 tablespoons of the oil into a shallow roasting pan large enough to hold the carp comfortably, and tip the pan back and forth to spread the oil evenly. Place the fish in the pan and brush the top with the remaining oil. Pour ¼ cup of the lemon-juice-and-water mixture over the fish and bake in the middle of the oven for 40 minutes, basting it every 15 minutes with the remaining lemon juice and water.

Serve at once from a heated platter.

Espada B'noua *(Morocco)*
SWORDFISH WITH LEMON JUICE AND ALMONDS

To serve 4

2 pounds swordfish, cut into four
½-inch-thick steaks
½ teaspoon salt
2 tablespoons butter, plus 2

tablespoons butter cut into bits
½ cup whole blanched almonds,
pulverized in a blender or nut
grinder
½ cup strained fresh lemon juice

Sprinkle both sides of the swordfish steaks lightly and evenly with the salt and set them aside.

In an 8- to 10-inch skillet, melt the 2 tablespoons of butter over moderate heat. When the foam begins to subside, drop in the almonds and, stirring almost constantly, cook for 3 to 5 minutes, or until they are lightly colored. Spread half the almonds in the bottom of a shallow casserole or flameproof baking-serving dish just large enough to hold the fish steaks in one layer. Arrange the fish on the bed of almonds, spread with the remaining almonds and dot the top with the bits of butter. Pour in the lemon juice and let it come to a boil over high heat. Immediately cover the pan, reduce the heat to low, and simmer gently for 10 to 12 minutes, or until the fish feels firm when prodded gently with a finger. Serve at once, directly from the baking dish or on individual heated plates.

Moules "Le Zoute" *(Belgium)*
BAKED MUSSELS WITH HERBS.

To serve 4

Rock salt or coarse salt *(see note, opposite)*
2 dozen large mussels (about 3 pounds), shucked, with the deeper half shell of each reserved
2 tablespoons finely chopped shallots
2 tablespoons finely chopped fresh parsley
1 teaspoon crumbled dried tarragon

½ teaspoon finely chopped garlic
½ teaspoon freshly ground black pepper
1½ cups soft fresh crumbs made from homemade-type white bread, pulverized in a blender or finely shredded with a fork
2 tablespoons butter, cut into small bits
1 lemon, cut lengthwise into quarters

Preheat the oven to 350°. Line a large shallow roasting pan or jelly-roll pan with rock salt (or coarse salt) to a depth of ½ inch. Scrub the reserved mussel shells thoroughly under cold running water, then pat them dry. Arrange them in a single layer in the salt-lined pan and place a mussel in each one. Combine the shallots, parsley, tarragon, garlic and pepper in a bowl and mix well. Then add the bread crumbs and toss thoroughly together. Sprinkle the top of the mussels evenly with the crumb-and-herb mixture, masking the mussels completely. Then dot each mussel with a few of the butter bits and bake in the middle of the oven for 10 minutes. Place the pan under a preheated broiler (about 3 inches from the heat) for a minute to brown the crumbs lightly. Transfer the mussels from the pan to a large heated platter, garnish with lemon and serve at once.

NOTE: The bed of salt is not indispensable to the success of this dish. You may, if you like, bake the mussels in any shallow baking dish large enough to hold the shells snugly in one layer.

Moules à l'Anversoise *(Belgium)*
MUSSELS IN HERB SAUCE

Mussels—like clams or oysters—must be purchased with tightly closed shells. If the shells of an open mussel do not close when run quickly under cold water, the mussel must not be used. If the shells do not open when cooked, they must be discarded.

To serve 4

3 pounds mussels in their shells (about 2 dozen)	chopped fresh parsley
10 tablespoons unsalted butter	2 tablespoons fresh chervil or 1 tablespoon crumbled, dried
½ cup finely chopped onions	chervil
½ cup finely chopped shallots	2 cups dry white wine
¼ cup plus 2 tablespoons finely	Freshly ground black pepper

Scrub the mussels thoroughly under cold running water with a stiff brush or soapless steel-mesh scouring pad. With a small, sharp knife scrape or pull the black ropelike tufts from the shells and discard them.

In a heavy 8-quart casserole, melt the butter over moderate heat. When the foam begins to subside, add the onions, shallots, ¼ cup of the parsley and the chervil. Stirring frequently, cook for about 5 minutes, or until the onions and shallots are soft and translucent but not brown. Watch carefully for any sign of burning and regulate the heat accordingly.

Stir in the wine and a few grindings of pepper, then add the mussels, placing them hinge side down. Cover the casserole tightly and bring to a boil over high heat. Reduce the heat to low and simmer for 5 to 7 minutes, until the mussels open, discarding those that remain closed. With a slotted spoon, transfer the mussels to a heated tureen or to individual serving bowls. Strain the stock through a fine sieve lined with a double thickness of dampened cheesecloth directly over the mussels. Sprinkle them with the remaining 2 tablespoons of parsley and serve at once.

Hut B'camoun (Morocco)

BAKED STRIPED BASS WITH CUMIN PASTE

To serve 4

A 3- to 3½-pound striped bass,
  cleaned but with head and tail
  left on
3 teaspoons salt
½ cup olive oil
½ cup finely chopped fresh parsley

2 tablespoons cumin seeds,
  pulverized in a blender or
  crushed with a mortar and pestle
2 tablespoons paprika
1 teaspoon finely chopped garlic
Freshly ground black pepper
1 lemon, cut crosswise into ⅛-inch-
  thick slices

Preheat the oven to 400°. Wash the fish under cold running water and rub it inside and out with 2 teaspoons of the salt. Let the fish rest at room temperature for 15 minutes, then wash it again under cold running water to remove the salt. Pat the fish completely dry with paper towels.

In a bowl, combine the oil, parsley, cumin, paprika, garlic, the remaining 1 teaspoon of salt and a few grindings of pepper. Stir until well mixed, then with your fingers spread the mixture evenly inside the cavity of the fish and over the surface of the skin, leaving only the head and tail exposed. Lay the fish on a large sheet of heavy-duty aluminum foil, fold the foil over the fish, and turn up the edges to enclose it completely. Place the wrapped fish on a baking sheet or jelly-roll pan and bake in the middle of the oven for about 40 minutes. The bass is done when its flesh feels firm when prodded gently with a finger. Do not overcook.

Before serving, open the foil and, using the ends as handles, carefully turn the fish out on a large, preferably preheated platter. Surround the fish with the lemon slices and serve at once.

Hut B'noua (Morocco)

RED SNAPPER WITH ALMOND PASTE

To serve 4 to 6

½ pound (1½ cups) blanched
  whole almonds
1 cup sugar
1 teaspoon cinnamon
1 teaspoon orange-blossom water
  (see Glossary)
2 tablespoons water
2 tablespoons oil
A 3- to 3½-pound red snapper,

cleaned but with head and tail
  left on
1 cup finely chopped onions
½ teaspoon pulverized saffron
  threads or powdered saffron
1 teaspoon salt
⅛ teaspoon freshly ground black
  pepper
2 tablespoons unsalted butter, cut
  into bits

Preheat the oven to 350°. Spread the nuts in a single layer in a jelly-roll pan and toast them in the oven for 8 to 10 minutes, turning them about frequently with a spoon. Watch carefully for any sign of burning. Transfer the nuts to an electric blender or a nut grinder and pulverize them with the sugar. Pour the mixture into a large bowl and stir in the cinnamon, orange-blossom water, water and oil. With a wooden spoon, mix and mash the ingredients to a smooth paste and set aside.

Raise the oven heat to 400°. Wash the fish inside and out with cold running water and dry it thoroughly with paper towels. Fill the cavity of the fish with half the almond paste, close the opening with small skewers, and crisscross kitchen string around them to secure them.

With a pastry brush, spread 1 tablespoon of oil over the bottom and sides of a baking-serving dish just large enough to hold the fish comfortably. Place the fish in the dish and surround it with the chopped onions. Sprinkle with saffron, salt and pepper; then, using a metal spatula, spread the remaining almond paste evenly over the top of the fish, leaving the head and tail exposed. Top with the bits of butter and bake in the center of the oven for 40 minutes, or until the fish feels firm when prodded gently with your finger. Serve at once, directly from the dish.

Schol uit de Oven (Netherlands)
FISH FILLETS "OUT OF THE OVEN"

To serve 6

6 five- to six-ounce skinned flounder fillets, each about ⅛ inch thick
1 tablespoon strained fresh lemon juice
2 teaspoons salt
3 tablespoons butter, softened
6 lean bacon slices
1 cup flour
¼ teaspoon dill seeds
¼ teaspoon ground nutmeg
Freshly ground black pepper
¼ cup freshly grated Gouda cheese
⅓ cup soft fresh crumbs made from homemade-type white bread, pulverized in a blender or finely shredded with a fork
¼ cup grated blanched almonds, pulverized in a blender or with a nut grinder
3 tablespoons chilled butter, cut into tiny bits

Pat the fillets completely dry with paper towels and sprinkle them on both sides with the lemon juice and salt. Set aside at room temperature for about 30 minutes.

Preheat the oven to 500°. With a pastry brush, spread 2 tablespoons of the softened butter over the bottom and sides of a shallow enameled or stainless-steel baking dish large enough to hold the fillets in one layer. Cut a piece of wax paper to fit snugly inside the dish and spread the remaining softened butter on one side of the paper. Set it aside.

In an 8- to 10-inch skillet, fry the bacon over moderate heat until it is lightly colored and begins to crisp. Transfer to paper towels to drain.

Continued on next page

Pat the fish fillets dry and fold them lengthwise in half, doubling them over. Press the edges together to hold them in shape. Dip the fish in the flour and shake each fillet gently to remove the excess flour. Sprinkle both sides of each fillet with the dill seeds and nutmeg. Arrange the fillets side by side in the buttered baking dish and lay a strip of bacon on each one. Grind a little pepper over the top. Combine the cheese, bread crumbs and almonds in a bowl and scatter the mixture evenly across the fish. Dot with the butter bits, then bake in the upper third of the oven for 10 minutes, or until the topping is brown and the fillets flake easily when prodded gently with a fork. Serve at once, directly from the baking dish.

Szczupak à la Polonaise (Poland)

POACHED FISH WITH HORSERADISH-AND-SOUR-CREAM SAUCE

To serve 4

2 cups coarsely chopped onions
1 medium-sized carrot, scraped and
    coarsely chopped
1 medium-sized parsnip, peeled and
    coarsely chopped
¼ celery root (celeriac), peeled
    and coarsely chopped
4 sprigs fresh parsley plus 1
    tablespoon finely chopped fresh
    parsley
4 whole allspice
2 medium-sized bay leaves
1 tablespoon plus ½ teaspoon salt
¼ cup plus 3 tablespoons distilled
    white vinegar
6 cups water

A 3- to 3½-pound pike or striped
    bass, cleaned and scaled, but with
    head and tail left on
6 medium-sized boiling potatoes
    (about 2 pounds), peeled and cut
    into 1-inch balls with a melon cutter
3 tablespoons butter, plus 2
    tablespoons butter chilled and cut
    into ¼-inch bits
3 tablespoons flour
1 cup sour cream
1 teaspoon sugar
¼ pound fresh horseradish, grated
    (⅓ cup), or substitute 4 ounces
    bottled grated white horseradish,
    thoroughly drained and squeezed
    dry in a towel
1 egg yolk

Combine the onions, carrot, parsnip, celery root, parsley sprigs, allspice, bay leaves and 1 tablespoon of the salt in a 3- to 4-quart enameled or stainless-steel saucepan. Pour in ¼ cup of the vinegar and the 6 cups of water, and bring to a boil over high heat. Reduce the heat to low and simmer partially covered for 45 minutes. Strain the liquid through a large fine sieve into a fish poacher or large, deep roasting pan, pressing down hard on the vegetables with the back of a spoon to extract all their juices before discarding them. Ladle ⅓ cup of the strained liquid into a cup or bowl and set it aside.

Wash the fish inside and out under cold running water. Without drying it, wrap the fish in a long, double-thick piece of dampened cheesecloth, leaving at least 6 inches of cloth at each end to serve as handles for lifting the fish. Twist the ends of the cloth close to the fish and tie them with string. Then place the fish on the rack of the poacher or roasting pan and lower it into the poacher or pan. (If you are using a roasting pan, tie the ends of the cheesecloth to the handles of the pan.) If necessary, add enough cold water to cover the fish by about 2 inches.

Cover the pan and bring to a boil over moderate heat; immediately reduce the heat to low and simmer slowly for about 20 minutes, or until the fish feels firm when prodded gently with a finger.

Using the ends of the cheesecloth as handles, lift the fish from the pan and lay it on a large cutting board or platter. Open the cheesecloth and skin the fish with a small, sharp knife by making a cut in the skin at the base of the tail and gently pulling off the skin in strips from tail to gill. Pick off and discard any bits of skin clinging to the cheesecloth. Holding both ends of the cheesecloth, carefully lift the fish and turn it over onto an ovenproof platter or shallow baking-serving dish. Peel off the skin on the upturned side and drape the fish loosely with aluminum foil. Set aside. Preheat the broiler to its highest possible setting.

Place the potato balls in a small saucepan and add enough cold water to cover them completely. Bring to a boil over high heat and cook briskly uncovered for about 12 minutes, or until the potatoes are tender and show no resistance when pierced deeply with the point of a small skewer or knife. Drain the potatoes and return them to the pan. Sliding the pan back and forth constantly over low heat, cook for 1 to 2 minutes, until the potatoes are dry. Cover the pan with a lid or foil to keep them warm.

In a heavy 8- to 10-inch skillet, melt 3 tablespoons of butter over moderate heat. When the foam begins to subside, add the flour and mix thoroughly with a wire whisk. Whisk in the reserved ⅓ cup of strained liquid and stir until the sauce comes to a boil, thickens heavily and is smooth. Reduce the heat to low and add the sour cream, sugar, horseradish, the remaining 3 tablespoons of vinegar and the remaining ½ teaspoon of salt. Whisking frequently, simmer for 3 or 4 minutes. In a small bowl, beat the egg yolk lightly with a fork and stir in 2 tablespoons of the simmering sauce. Stirring constantly with the whisk, pour the egg mixture back into the main sauce in a slow, thin stream. Immediately remove the sauce from the heat and taste for seasoning.

Pour the sauce over the fish and spread it smoothly with a spatula to mask the fish completely. Scatter the 2 tablespoons of butter bits on top and slide the fish under the broiler, 3 or 4 inches from the heat. Broil for 2 to 3 minutes, until the sauce is delicately browned, watching it constantly to make sure it does not burn.

Arrange the potato balls attractively around the fish, sprinkle them with parsley, and serve at once.

To debone the fish for serving, divide the top layer into 2 portions with a fish server without cutting through the spine. Leave the head and tail intact. Lift the portions with the server and a fork and arrange them attractively on serving plates. Then gently remove the backbone in one piece, discard it and divide the bottom layer of fish into individual portions as before.

Poultry and Game

Tajine Msir Zitun *(Morocco)*
CHICKEN WITH LEMON AND OLIVES

To serve 4

4 tablespoons olive oil
A 3- to 3½-pound chicken, cut
   into 8 serving pieces
1 cup finely chopped onions
2 teaspoons imported paprika
1 teaspoon ground ginger
¼ teaspoon turmeric

1 teaspoon salt
Freshly ground black pepper
2 salted lemons *(page 99)*, cut into
   quarters, or substitute 2 fresh
   lemons, cut lengthwise into
   quarters and seeded
1 cup water
24 small green olives

In a heavy 12-inch skillet, warm the oil over high heat until a light haze forms above it. Brown the chicken in the hot oil, four pieces at a time, turning them frequently with tongs or a slotted spoon and regulating the heat so they color richly and evenly without burning. As they brown, transfer the chicken pieces to a plate.

Pour off all but a thin film of fat from the skillet and add the onions. Stirring frequently, cook for 8 to 10 minutes, until the onions are soft and brown. Watch carefully for any sign of burning and regulate the heat accordingly. Stir in the paprika, ginger, turmeric, salt and a few grindings of pepper. Add the fresh lemons (if you are using them), the chicken and the liquid that has accumulated around it, and pour in the water. Bring to a boil over high heat, then reduce the heat to low and simmer covered for 30 minutes, or until the chicken is tender and shows no resistance when a thigh is pierced deeply with a small skewer or knife. Then add the olives and the salted lemon quarters (if you are using them), cover, and simmer for 4 or 5 minutes, until the lemons and olives are heated through. Taste for seasoning.

To serve, arrange the chicken pieces attractively on a deep platter and place the lemon quarters and olives in a ring around them. Pour the sauce over the chicken and serve at once.

Minina *(Tunisia)*
BAKED CHICKEN OMELET

To serve 6

1 calf's brain (about 8 ounces)
1 tablespoon white distilled vinegar
2 teaspoons strained fresh lemon
   juice
1 1-2 teaspoons salt
A 1-pound chicken breast

9 eggs
3 hard-cooked eggs, finely chopped
1-8 teaspoon ground nutmeg,
   preferably freshly grated
Freshly ground black pepper
1-4 cup vegetable oil
1 lemon, cut lengthwise into 6
   wedges

Soak the brain in several changes of cold water for 2 hours; then soak it for another hour in 1 quart of cold water combined with 1 tablespoon of vinegar. Gently pull off as much of the outside membrane as possible without tearing the brain and cut off the white, opaque bits at the base with a small, sharp knife. Place the brain in a small enameled saucepan, add 3 cups of water, the lemon juice and ½ teaspoon of the salt. Bring to a simmer over moderate heat and poach uncovered for about 5 minutes. Place the brain on paper towels and pat it completely dry. Then cut it into approximately 1-inch pieces.

Place the chicken breast in an 8- to 10-inch skillet and add enough water to cover it by about 1 inch. Add ½ teaspoon of the salt. Bring to a boil over high heat, meanwhile skimming off the foam and scum that rise to the surface. Reduce the heat to low and poach the chicken partially covered for about 15 minutes, or until the breast feels firm to the touch. Drain the chicken, reserving the poaching liquid With a small knife, remove the skin and bones from the breast and discard them. Cut the chicken into pieces about ½ inch wide and 1 inch long.

Preheat the oven to 350°. In a deep bowl, beat the 9 eggs with a whisk or fork until they are well mixed. Add the brains, chicken pieces and hard-cooked eggs and fold together gently but thoroughly. Stir in the nutmeg, the remaining ½ teaspoon of salt and a liberal grinding of pepper.

Pour the oil into a deep 6- to 7-inch skillet with an ovenproof handle and warm it over high heat until the oil is very hot but not smoking. Add the egg mixture and bake uncovered in the middle of the oven for 15 minutes, or until a knife inserted in the center of the omelet comes out clean. Reheat the reserved chicken poaching stock.

To unmold and serve the omelet, run a thin-bladed knife around the sides to loosen them and invert a heated serving plate over the skillet. Grasping plate and skillet together firmly, turn them over. The omelet should slide out easily. Sprinkle about ¼ cup of the chicken stock evenly over the omelet to moisten it, and arrange the lemon wedges around the edge of the plate. Cut the omelet into pie-shaped wedges and serve either hot or at room temperature.

Pollo alla Campagna *(Switzerland)*

CHICKEN WITH TOMATO SAUCE AND BACON

To serve 4

A 3- to 3½-pound chicken, cut
   into 8 serving pieces
1 teaspoon salt
Freshly ground black pepper
1 cup all-purpose flour
3 to 5 tablespoons butter
2 to 4 tablespoons olive oil

½ pound thinly sliced lean bacon,
   cut crosswise into 2-inch pieces
¼ cup finely chopped shallots
4 medium-sized firm ripe tomatoes,
   peeled, seeded and coarsely
   chopped *(see bigos, page 80)*
¾ cup dry white wine, preferably
   Neuchâtel or Fendant

Pat the chicken completely dry with paper towels. Sprinkle the pieces on all sides with the salt and a few grindings of pepper. Then coat the chicken with flour and shake each piece vigorously to remove any excess.

In a heavy 10- to 12-inch skillet, melt 3 tablespoons of the butter with 2 tablespoons of the oil over high heat. When the foam begins to subside, brown the chicken in the hot fat, 4 pieces at a time. Start the pieces skin side down and turn them frequently with tongs or a slotted spoon until they are richly and evenly colored. As they brown, transfer the pieces to a plate and brown the rest of the chicken similarly, adding the remaining butter and oil to the pan if necessary. Pour off the fat remaining in the skillet and in its place add the bacon. Stirring frequently, cook over moderate heat until the bacon is crisp and brown and has rendered all its fat. With a slotted spoon, remove the bacon to paper towels to drain. Add the shallots to the bacon fat in the skillet and, stirring constantly, cook for about 3 minutes, or until they are soft, transparent and lightly brown. Add the tomatoes and wine and, stirring from time to time, cook briskly, uncovered, over high heat until most of the liquid in the pan has evaporated and the mixture is thick enough to hold its shape lightly in a spoon.

Return the chicken and bacon to the skillet and turn them about with a spoon until they are well coated with the tomato sauce. Bring to a boil, reduce the heat to low, and simmer partially covered for 35 to 40 minutes. When the chicken is done it should show no resistance when a thigh is pierced with a small, sharp knife. Taste the sauce for seasoning.

With tongs, remove the chicken from the skillet and arrange the pieces skin side up on a large heated platter. Pour the sauce over the chicken and serve at once.

Djeja M'qalia (Morocco)
CHICKEN WITH CORIANDER AND MINT

To serve 4

2 teaspoons finely chopped garlic	½ teaspoon powdered cumin
1 tablespoon paprika	1 to 2 tablespoons vegetable oil
¼ teaspoon pulverized saffron threads or powdered saffron	A 3- to 3½-pound chicken
	2 teaspoons salt
¼ cup finely chopped fresh coriander (cilantro) leaves	Freshly ground black pepper
	1 cup coarsely chopped onions
¼ cup finely chopped fresh mint	1 cup water

In a small bowl combine the garlic, paprika, saffron, coriander, mint, cumin and 1 tablespoon of oil. With a wooden spoon, mix and mash the ingredients to a paste that is dense enough to hold its shape lightly in a spoon. If the paste seems too dry, stir in up to 1 tablespoon more of oil by the teaspoonful.

Pat the chicken completely dry with paper towels and sprinkle it inside and out with the salt and a few grindings of black pepper.

Preheat the oven to 375°. With your fingers, rub the entire surface of the chicken with the herb paste, patting and spreading it as evenly as possible. Place the chicken in a heavy 4- to 6-quart casserole, surround it with the chopped onions, and pour 1 cup of water down one side of the pot, without getting any water on the chicken.

Cover the casserole and bring to a boil over high heat. Then braise in the center of the oven for about 45 minutes. To test if the chicken is done, pierce a thigh with the point of a small, sharp knife. The juices that run out should be pale yellow; if the juices are pink, braise 10 to 15 minutes longer. Transfer the chicken from the casserole to a plate and keep the braising juices warm.

Preheat the broiler to its highest point, or light a layer of coals in a charcoal broiler and let them burn until a white ash appears on the surface. Broil the chicken 3 inches from the heat for about 6 to 8 minutes, turning it frequently with 2 wooden spoons, until it is richly and evenly browned on all sides.

Serve the chicken at once, accompanied by the heated braising sauce in a sauceboat or bowl.

Tâham bel Djedje ouel Khodra (Algeria)
STEAMED COUSCOUS WITH CHICKEN AND VEGETABLES

To serve 6

COUSCOUS
2 pounds *couscous (see Glossary)*
2½ teaspoons salt dissolved in
   2½ cups cold water

1 tablespoon olive oil
4 tablespoons unsalted butter, cut
   into bits
¼ teaspoon ground cinnamon

Spread the *couscous* evenly in a large shallow pan. Sprinkle it with 2 cups of the salt water, then dribble 1 tablespoon of olive oil over the top. Rub the moistened grains gently between your palms, lifting and dropping the *couscous* back into the pan, until the water and oil have been completely absorbed. Cover the pan with foil or plastic wrap and set the *couscous* aside at room temperature for 15 to 20 minutes; the pellets will swell slightly.

CHICKEN AND VEGETABLES
4 tablespoons olive oil
A 2½- to 3-pound chicken, cut
   into 12 pieces and patted dry with
   paper towels
1 medium-sized red onion, peeled
   and finely grated
½ teaspoon ground cinnamon
1 tablespoon salt
1 teaspoon freshly ground black
   pepper
4 cups cold water
½ pound (about 1 cup) dried
   chick-peas *(garbanzos)*, soaked
   for 12 hours, drained, rinsed,

simmered in water to cover for
   1 hour and drained again, or
   substitute 2 cups drained canned
   chick-peas
4 medium-sized carrots (about
   1 pound), scraped and cut into
   2-inch lengths
1½ pounds medium-sized white
   turnips, peeled and each cut
   lengthwise into quarters
1½ pounds medium-sized
   zucchini, peeled and each cut
   lengthwise into quarters
1 teaspoon *hrisa* (optional; *page 103)*

Meanwhile, in the lower part of a 4-quart *couscoussier* or in a deep 6-quart kettle or casserole, combine 4 tablespoons of olive oil, the chicken, grated onion, ½ teaspoon cinnamon, 1 tablespoon salt and the pepper. Fry uncovered over high heat for about 10 minutes, frequently turning the chicken over with tongs until the pieces are golden brown on all sides. Add 4 cups of cold water (or just enough to cover the chicken) and the chick-peas, and stir until the mixture comes to a boil. Reduce the heat to moderate.

Set the top part of the *couscoussier* in place. Or set a colander lined with cheesecloth in the kettle or casserole; it should not touch the food in the pot. Twist damp paper towels or kitchen towels into long narrow strips and wrap them around the rim of the *couscoussier* or kettle to seal the joint between the upper and lower parts.

Slowly add about 2 cups of the *couscous* to the upper pot or colander, rubbing the pellets between your palms as you drop them in, and letting them mound naturally. When steam begins to rise through the pellets, add another cup or so of *couscous* in the same manner. Repeat, letting steam appear after each addition. When all the *couscous* has been rubbed into the pot, continue to steam uncovered and undisturbed for 20 minutes. Remove the top part of the *couscoussier,* return the *couscous* to the shallow pan, spread it out with a wooden spoon, and set aside.

When the chicken is tender but not falling apart, transfer it with tongs to a platter and drape foil over it to keep it warm. Add the carrots and turnips to the stew and pour in enough boiling water to cover the vegetables completely. Stirring occasionally, bring to a boil over high heat. Reduce the heat to moderate, set the top pot (or colander) in place again, and let the vegetables cook while you complete the *couscous.*

Sprinkle the remaining ½ cup of salt water, the butter bits and ¼ teaspoon of cinnamon over the *couscous* and rub the grains gently between your palms as before until the water and butter are completely absorbed.

Again seal the joint at the rim of the pot with the towel strips. Slowly add 2 cups of the *couscous* to the top part of the pot as you did before, rubbing the pellets between your palms as you drop them in, letting them mound naturally, and waiting for steam to appear before adding more. Steam uncovered and undisturbed for about 15 minutes, or until the carrots and turnips are tender but not falling apart. Transfer them with a slotted spoon to the reserved chicken, add the zucchini to the pot, and replace the top. Continue steaming the *couscous* undisturbed for another 10 to 15 minutes, or until it is soft but still somewhat resistant to the bite.

To serve, mound the *couscous* on a large heated platter. Return the chicken and vegetables to the stew and cook over high heat for 2 to 3 minutes, until it is heated through. Taste for seasoning and add *hrisa* to the stew if desired. Moisten the *couscous* with about 1 cup of the sauce and arrange the chicken attractively on top. Place the vegetables in a ring around the *couscous.* Pour the remaining sauce into a bowl and present it separately. Serve at once.

Sferia *(Algeria)*

CHICKEN WITH CHICK-PEAS AND CHEESE CROQUETTES

To serve 4

2 tablespoons butter

A 3- to 3½-pound chicken, cut into 8 serving pieces

1 small onion, peeled and finely grated

½ teaspoon ground cinnamon

1 teaspoon salt

Freshly ground black pepper

1 cup dried chick-peas *(garbanzos)*, soaked 12 hours, drained, rinsed, simmered in water to cover for 1 hour and drained again, or substitute 2 cups drained canned chick-peas

1 cup water

In a heavy 3- to 4-quart casserole, combine the butter, chicken, onion, ½ teaspoon cinnamon, 1 teaspoon salt and several grindings of black pepper. Turning the chicken frequently, cook uncovered over high heat for about 15 minutes, or until it is golden on all sides. Add the chick-peas and water and, stirring constantly, bring to a boil over high heat. Reduce the heat to low and simmer covered for 1½ hours, or until the chicken is tender but not falling apart.

CROQUETTES

1 small (½ pound) loaf fresh French- or Italian-type white bread, trimmed of all crusts and torn into ½-inch pieces

¼ cup milk

1 egg plus 1 egg yolk

1 cup freshly grated imported Gruyère cheese

1 teaspoon orange-blossom water *(see Glossary)*

¼ teaspoon ground cinnamon

¼ teaspoon salt

1 cup vegetable oil

Meanwhile, preheat the oven to its lowest setting. Line a large shallow baking pan with a double thickness of paper towels and place it in the middle of the oven. Combine the bread and milk in a deep bowl, soak for 10 minutes, then squeeze the bread vigorously to rid it of all moisture. Discard the milk and return the bread to the bowl. Add the egg and egg yolk, and stir with a fork or spoon until the ingredients are well blended. Stir in the cheese, orange-blossom water, ¼ teaspoon cinnamon and ¼ teaspoon salt, and beat until the mixture is smooth. Taste for seasoning.

In a heavy 10-inch skillet warm the oil over high heat until a light haze forms above it. Moistening your hands frequently with cold water, shape the croquette mixture into about 2 dozen slightly flattened balls, each about 1 inch in diameter. Fry the croquettes 5 or 6 at a time in the hot oil for 1 or 2 minutes on each side, turning them with a slotted spatula. As they brown, transfer them to the paper-lined pan and keep them warm in the oven while you fry the rest in similar batches, adding more oil to the pan as necessary.

SAUCE
1 egg yolk
1 tablespoon strained fresh lemon

juice
2 tablespoons finely chopped fresh
    parsley

When the chicken is done, arrange the cheese croquettes in a ring around the edge of a large serving platter and place the pieces of chicken in another ring inside them. Remove the chick-peas from the casserole with a slotted spoon and mound them in the center. Drape the platter loosely with foil and return to the oven to keep warm while you make the sauce. Working quickly, beat the egg yolk and lemon juice together with a fork or whisk until they are well combined, beat in ½ cup of the sauce from the casserole, and then pour the egg mixture into the remaining sauce. Stirring constantly, cook over low heat until the sauce thickens lightly. Do not let it come to a boil or it will curdle. Taste for seasoning and pour the sauce over the chick-peas and chicken. Sprinkle the top with the parsley and serve at once.

Lapin à la Flamande (Belgium)
RABBIT IN PRUNE SAUCE

To serve 6

¾ cup (about 4 ounces) seedless
    raisins
12 pitted dried prunes
⅓ cup cognac
A 4- to 4½-pound rabbit, cut into
    small serving pieces
1 tablespoon salt
Freshly ground black pepper

¼ pound slab bacon, cut in ¼-
    inch dice
2 tablespoons butter
12 small white onions, each about 1
    inch in diameter, peeled
1 tablespoon flour
1¾ cups water
¼ teaspoon thyme
1 tablespoon sugar
1 tablespoon red wine vinegar

Combine the raisins, prunes and cognac in a small bowl and set them aside to marinate at room temperature for at least 3 hours. If the cognac does not cover the fruit completely, stir gently from time to time to keep all the fruit well moistened.

Pat the pieces of rabbit completely dry with paper towels and sprinkle them on all sides with the salt and a few grindings of pepper. In a heavy 4- to 4½-quart casserole, fry the diced bacon over moderate heat, stirring occasionally. When the dice are crisp and have rendered all their fat transfer them to paper towels with a slotted spoon.

Pour off and discard all but about 3 tablespoons of the bacon fat and add 2 tablespoons of butter to the casserole. Melt the butter over high

Continued on next page

heat and brown the rabbit in the hot fat, a few pieces at a time, turning them frequently with tongs or a slotted spoon and regulating the heat so that they color richly and evenly without burning. As they brown, transfer the rabbit pieces to a plate.

Pour off all but about 2 tablespoons of the fat remaining in the casserole and drop in the small white onions. Sliding the casserole back and forth frequently to roll the onions around, fry for about 8 minutes, or until they are golden brown. With a slotted spoon, transfer the onions to a separate plate.

Stir 1 tablespoon of flour into the fat remaining in the casserole. Then pour in 1½ cups of the water and bring to a boil over high heat, stirring constantly with a rubber spatula and scraping in the brown particles that cling to the bottom and sides of the pan.

Add the thyme and the reserved bacon dice. Return the pieces of rabbit and any liquid that has accumulated around them to the casserole. Turn the pieces about until they are thoroughly moistened. Reduce the heat to low and cover the casserole with both a sheet of foil and the casserole lid to seal it as tightly as possible.

Simmer the rabbit for 1 hour. Then add the reserved onions and stir in the raisins, prunes and cognac. Simmer tightly covered for about 1 hour longer, or until the rabbit is tender and shows no resistance when pierced with the point of a small, sharp knife.

With a slotted spoon, transfer the pieces of rabbit to a heated deep platter and arrange the onions, raisins and prunes attractively around it. Drape the platter loosely with aluminum foil to help keep the rabbit warm while you prepare the sauce.

In a small enameled saucepan or skillet, bring the sugar and the remaining ¼ cup of water to a boil over high heat. Stirring constantly with a metal spoon, cook briskly, uncovered, until the syrup begins to caramelize and turns a golden tealike brown. Still stirring, pour in the red wine vinegar and gradually stir in about ½ cup of the liquid remaining in the casserole.

Pour the entire contents of the saucepan or skillet back into the casserole and, still stirring constantly, simmer the sauce over low heat for one or two minutes. Taste the sauce for seasoning, then pour it over the rabbit and serve at once.

Shoua *(Morocco)*
STEAMED CHICKEN STUFFED WITH SWEETENED COUSCOUS

To serve 4

2 cups leftover steamed *couscous*
   (pages 42, 78 and 82)
2 tablespoons seedless raisins
2 tablespoons coarsely chopped
   blanched almonds
2 tablespoons coarsely chopped
   walnuts
1 tablespoon unsalted butter,
   melted, plus 3 tablespoons
   unsalted butter

1 tablespoon honey
⅛ teaspoon ground cinnamon
⅛ teaspoon turmeric
A pinch of ground ginger
A pinch of ground cumin
A pinch of ground cloves
Freshly ground black pepper
A 3-pound chicken
½ teaspoon salt
3 tablespoons vegetable oil

In a deep bowl, combine the *couscous,* raisins, almonds, walnuts, melted butter, honey, cinnamon, turmeric, ginger, cumin, cloves and a few grindings of pepper. Stir until the ingredients are thoroughly mixed.

Pat the chicken completely dry with paper towels and sprinkle it inside and out with the salt. Stuff the cavity with the *couscous* mixture, and close the opening by lacing it with small skewers and kitchen cord or by sewing it with a large needle and heavy white thread. Fasten the neck skin to the back with a skewer and truss the bird securely.

Pour enough boiling water into the lower part of a steamer to come to within an inch of the cooking rack and place the chicken on the rack. Bring the water to a boil again, reduce the heat to moderate, cover the steamer tightly, and steam the bird for 45 minutes. To test for doneness, pierce the thigh with the point of a small skewer or sharp knife. The juice that trickles out should be pale yellow; if it is tinged with pink, steam the chicken for another 5 to 10 minutes. Remove the chicken from the steamer and pat it thoroughly dry with paper towels.

If you do not have a steamer, you can improvise one by pouring boiling water into a large 6- to 8-quart pot to a depth of about 2 inches. Place two or three small heatproof bowls or custard cups right side up in the pot and set a shallow baking dish on top of them. There must be enough space around the edges of the dish to allow the steam to rise and circulate freely. Place the chicken in the baking dish and steam it, following the directions above.

In a heavy 10- to 12-inch skillet, melt the remaining 3 tablespoons of butter in the oil over high heat. When a light haze forms above it, add the chicken. Turn it frequently with tongs or a slotted spoon and regulate the heat so that the bird colors richly and evenly on all sides without burning. Transfer the chicken to a heated platter and serve at once.

L'Oie à l'Instar de Visé (Belgium)
POACHED GOOSE WITH WHITE GARLIC SAUCE

To serve 4 to 8

A 10- to 11-pound goose, cut into quarters and trimmed of excess fat

The goose's giblets: gizzard, heart and liver

3 quarts cold water

2 whole heads of garlic, unpeeled

2 medium-sized carrots, scraped

2 celery stalks, including the leaves

2 medium-sized onions, peeled

1 medium-sized leek, including 2 inches of the green top, trimmed and thoroughly washed to rid it of all sand

A bouquet of 6 fresh parsley sprigs and 1 medium-sized bay leaf, tied together

½ teaspoon crumbled dried thyme

1 teaspoon salt

4 tablespoons flour

3 egg yolks

¾ cup heavy cream

Combine the goose quarters, the giblets and the cold water in a heavy 8-quart casserole and bring to a boil over high heat, meanwhile skimming off and discarding the scum and foam as they rise to the surface. Add the garlic, carrots, celery, onions, leek, the bouquet, thyme and salt, and reduce the heat to low. Partially cover the casserole and simmer the goose for about 1½ hours, or until the flesh of a thigh shows no resistance when pierced with the point of a small, sharp knife. Then with tongs or a slotted spoon, remove the heads of garlic and set them aside. Transfer the goose quarters to a carving board. Cut away and discard the backbone and cut the goose into 8 serving pieces, trimming away any excess fat. Strain the remaining contents of the casserole through a sieve set over a deep bowl and discard the vegetables. Let the stock settle for a few minutes; then, with a large spoon, skim as much fat as possible from the surface and reserve it in a separate bowl. Peel the garlic, rub the cloves through a fine sieve with the back of a spoon and set the purée aside.

In a heavy 10- to 12-inch skillet, heat ¼ cup of the reserved goose fat until it is very hot but not smoking. Add the pieces of goose, a few at a time, and turn them frequently with tongs. As they brown, arrange the pieces skin side up on a heated platter. Drape a sheet of foil loosely over the goose to keep it warm while you make the sauce.

In a heavy 1½- to 2-quart saucepan, heat 3 tablespoons of the remaining goose fat over moderate heat. Stir in the flour and mix together thoroughly. Pour in 4 cups of the goose stock, add the puréed garlic and, stirring constantly with a whisk, cook over high heat until the sauce comes to a boil and thickens. Reduce the heat to low and simmer uncovered for about 5 minutes to remove any taste of raw flour. Then combine the egg yolks and cream in a bowl and beat in about ½ cup of the simmering sauce. Pour this back into the sauce in a thin stream, whisking constantly. Simmer for 1 to 2 minutes longer, then taste for seasoning, pour the sauce over the goose, and serve at once.

Ratza ala Romania
BRAISED DUCK WITH CABBAGE

To serve 4

A 1-pound white cabbage
¼ pound lean slab bacon, cut into ¼-inch dice
A 5-pound duck, cut into 8 serving pieces
¼ cup finely chopped fresh fennel, or substitute ½ teaspoon powdered fennel
2 tablespoons finely chopped

shallots, or substitute 2 tablespoons finely chopped scallions, white parts only
½ teaspoon finely chopped garlic
½ teaspoon crumbled dried thyme
¼ teaspoon crumbled dried sage
¼ teaspoon crumbled dried marjoram
1½ cups sauerkraut juice

Remove the tough outer leaves of the cabbage, wash the head under cold running water, and cut it into quarters. Shred the cabbage by cutting out the core, then slicing the quarters crosswise in ⅛-inch-wide strips.

In a heavy 4- to 6-quart casserole, fry the bacon over moderate heat, stirring frequently until the bits are brown and crisp and have rendered most of their fat. With a slotted spoon, transfer the bacon bits to paper towels to drain. Pour all but 2 tablespoons of the fat remaining in the casserole into a cup or bowl and set aside.

With paper towels pat the pieces of duck completely dry. Then brown them in the casserole, 3 or 4 at a time, turning them frequently with tongs. As they brown, transfer the pieces of duck to a plate.

Preheat the oven to 425°. Discard all the fat in the casserole and in its place add the reserved bacon fat. Drop in the shredded cabbage, fennel, shallots or scallions, garlic, thyme, sage and marjoram. Stirring frequently, cook uncovered over moderate heat until the cabbage is limp but not brown. Add the sauerkraut juice and stir until it comes to a boil.

Arrange the pieces of duck on top of the cabbage, pour in the liquid that has accumulated around them, and scatter the reserved bacon bits over the top. Cover the casserole tightly and braise in the lowest part of the oven for 15 minutes. Lower the heat to 325° and continue to braise for about 1 hour longer, or until the duck is tender.

With a long spoon skim off and discard all the surface fat and serve the duck and cabbage directly from the casserole. Or mound the cabbage on a deep heated platter and arrange the duck pieces over or around it.

La Grive à la Liégeoise (Belgium)
QUAIL WITH JUNIPER BERRIES

The traditional Belgian recipe is for thrush (grive), which is generally un-available in the United States; quail is an excellent alternative.

To serve 4

4 oven-ready quail (about 4 to
    5 ounces each)
Salt
Freshly ground black pepper
8 tablespoons (1 quarter-pound
    stick) unsalted butter
5 tablespoons vegetable oil
16 juniper berries
2 tablespoons gin
¼ cup chicken stock, fresh or
    canned

⅓ cup finely chopped celery
⅓ cup finely chopped leeks, white
    part only
⅓ cup finely chopped scraped
    carrots
¼ cup finely chopped scraped
    turnips
¼ cup finely chopped onions
⅛ teaspoon sugar
4 thin slices homemade-type white
    bread, cut into 4-inch rounds

Wash the birds under cold running water and pat them completely dry inside and out with paper towels. With your fingers rub the cavity of each bird with a little salt and pepper and tie the legs together with string.

In a heavy 10- to 12-inch skillet, melt 2 tablespoons of the butter with 1 tablespoon of the oil over moderate heat. When the foam subsides and the fat begins to color very lightly, add the juniper berries and birds and, turning them frequently with tongs or a spoon, brown them delicately on all sides. Regulate the heat as necessary so that the birds color evenly without burning. Warm the gin in a small pan over low heat, ignite it with a match and pour it flaming over the birds a little at a time, sliding the skillet back and forth over the heat until the flames die.

Transfer the birds to a platter and pour the chicken stock into the skillet. Bring to a boil over high heat, stirring constantly and scraping in the brown particles that cling to the bottom and sides of the pan. Then cook briskly until the liquid is reduced to about 2 tablespoons. Remove the pan from the heat and set it aside.

In a heavy 4- to 5-quart casserole, melt 2 tablespoons of the remaining butter over moderate heat. Add the celery, leeks, carrots, turnip, onions and sugar, and, stirring frequently, cook for about 5 minutes, or until the vegetables are soft but not brown. Arrange the birds on their backs on the bed of vegetables and pour the reserved liquid from the skillet into the casserole. Cover tightly and cook over low heat for about 30 minutes, basting the birds with their cooking juices after the first 15 minutes. Test the birds for doneness by lifting one up and tilting it over the pot. The juice that runs out of the cavity should be clear yellow. If it shows any touch of pink, cook the birds 5 to 10 minutes longer.

Leave the finished birds in the casserole (off the heat) while you heat the remaining 4 tablespoons of butter and the remaining 4 tablespoons of oil in a large skillet. Fry the bread rounds until they are crisp and golden brown. Then arrange the rounds on a heated platter and place a bird on each round. Pour the remaining contents of the casserole through a fine sieve into a bowl, pressing down firmly on the vegetables with the back of a spoon. Skim the sauce of excess fat, taste for seasoning, then spoon it over the birds. Serve at once.

Pilaf s Padpadutsi i Stafidi *(Bulgaria)*
PILAF OF QUAIL WITH CURRANTS

To serve 4

4 one-pound oven-ready quail	1 teaspoon finely chopped garlic
2 teaspoons salt	1½ cups long-grain unconverted
Freshly ground black pepper	white rice
5 tablespoons butter	3 cups cold water
1 tablespoon vegetable oil	¼ cup dried currants
½ cup finely chopped onions	¼ cup dried white raisins

Preheat the oven to 350°. Wash the quail under running water and pat them completely dry inside and out with paper towels. Sprinkle the cavities of the birds with 1 teaspoon of salt and a few grindings of pepper.

In a heavy 3- to 4-quart casserole, melt 2 tablespoons of the butter with the oil over high heat. When the foam begins to subside, brown the birds in the hot fat, turning them frequently with tongs and regulating the heat so that they color richly and evenly without burning. Be careful not to crowd the pot; if necessary brown the quail two at a time. As they brown, transfer the birds to a plate. Add the remaining 3 tablespoons of butter to the casserole, drop in the onions and garlic and, stirring frequently, fry for about 5 minutes. When the onions are soft and golden, pour in the rice and stir for 2 or 3 minutes, until the grains glisten with the butter. Mix in the water, currants, raisins and the remaining teaspoon of salt, and bring to a boil over high heat.

Arrange the quail on top of the rice, and moisten the birds with any liquid that has accumulated on the plate. Cover the casserole tightly and bake in the middle of the oven for about 15 to 20 minutes, or until all the liquid has been absorbed by the rice. To test the quail for doneness, pierce the thigh with the point of a small, sharp knife. The juice that trickles out should be pale yellow with no trace of pink; if necessary, return the casserole to the oven and cook for 5 to 10 minutes longer.

Serve at once, directly from the casserole, or fluff the pilaf with a fork and mound it on a heated platter, then arrange the quail around it.

Bastila *(Morocco)*
FLAKY PIGEON PIE

To serve 4 to 6

4 one-pound oven-ready pigeons, with wing tips removed, or substitute 4 one-pound squab chickens

Salt

Freshly ground black pepper

12 tablespoons (1½ quarter-pound sticks) unsalted butter

1 cup finely chopped onions

The pigeon or chicken hearts, gizzards and livers, finely chopped

2 tablespoons finely chopped fresh coriander *(cilantro)*

1 tablespoon finely chopped fresh parsley

1 teaspoon ground ginger

½ teaspoon ground cumin

½ teaspoon ground hot red pepper (cayenne)

¼ teaspoon turmeric

⅛ teaspoon crumbled saffron threads or ground saffron

⅛ teaspoon plus ½ teaspoon cinnamon

1 cup water

6 eggs plus 2 egg yolks

1½ cups blanched almonds

2 tablespoons sugar

18 *malsouqua (page 106)*, or substitute 10 sheets *filo* pastry *(see Glossary)*, each about 16 inches long and 12 inches wide, thoroughly defrosted if frozen

8 tablespoons (1 quarter-pound stick) unsalted butter, melted

3 tablespoons unsalted butter combined with 3 tablespoons vegetable oil

2 tablespoons confectioners' sugar combined with 1 tablespoon cinnamon

Pat the birds thoroughly dry inside and out with paper towels and sprinkle the cavities and skin with ½ teaspoon of salt and a few grindings of pepper. In a heavy 12-inch skillet, melt 8 tablespoons of the butter over moderate heat. When the foam begins to subside, brown the pigeons in the hot fat, turning them frequently with tongs or a slotted spoon and regulating the heat so they color richly and evenly on all sides without burning. As they brown, transfer the birds to a plate.

Add the onions and the pigeon or chicken hearts, gizzards and livers to the fat remaining in the skillet and, stirring frequently, cook for about 5 minutes, or until the onions are soft and translucent but not brown. Stir in the coriander, parsley, ginger, cumin, red pepper, turmeric, saffron and ⅛ teaspoon of cinnamon. Add the cup of water and bring to a boil over high heat, stirring constantly. Then return the birds and the liquid that has accumulated around them to the skillet, and reduce the heat to low. Cover and simmer for about 1 hour, or until the birds are tender and show no resistance when a thigh is pierced deeply with the point of a small knife. Transfer the birds to a platter and, when they are cool enough to handle, with a sharp knife remove and discard the skin and bones. Cut the meat into strips about 2 inches long and 1 inch wide.

Pour 1½ cups of the sauce remaining in the skillet into a bowl and set aside. Bring the rest of the sauce to a boil over high heat and, stirring from time to time, cook briskly until it is reduced to about 4 tablespoons of glaze. As the fat rises to the surface of the boiling sauce, skim it off with a spoon and discard it. With a rubber spatula, scrape the glaze into a small bowl and return the reserved 1½ cups of sauce to the skillet.

Beat the eggs and egg yolks with a whisk or fork until they are combined, but do not overbeat them. Stirring the sauce in the skillet constantly, pour in the eggs and cook over moderate heat until the mixture forms soft, creamy curds. Remove the skillet from the heat and stir in the glaze. Taste for seasoning and set aside.

Melt 4 tablespoons of butter in a small skillet over moderate heat. When the foam begins to subside, add the almonds and, stirring frequently, fry them for about 5 minutes, or until they are lightly and evenly browned. Drain the almonds on paper towels, then chop them coarsely. In a small bowl, combine the chopped almonds, 2 tablespoons of sugar and ½ teaspoon of cinnamon.

To assemble the *bastila* with *malsouqua*, arrange 6 of the pastries on a flat surface, overlapping them in a large circle, then top with 6 more, overlapping as before. Stack 4 more pastries in the center. (To assemble the pie with *filo*, overlap 6 sheets of *filo* in a circle, fold 2 sheets in half and place them one atop the other in the center of the circle.) Sprinkle the almond-sugar-and-cinnamon mixture in a 9-inch-wide circle in the center of the pastry and spread it with half of the egg-sauce mixture. Top this with strips of pigeon or chicken meat arranged in one layer and cover with the remaining egg-sauce mixture. With a pastry brush, coat the exposed borders of the pastry lightly with the melted butter. One at a time, bring the 6 intermediate circles of *malsouqua* or 2 folded sheets of *filo* up over the filling, brushing each again with butter as you proceed. Top the center of the pie with 2 more circles of *malsouqua* or folded sheets of *filo*, and bring up the bottom layer of *malsouqua* or *filo* to enclose the pie.

In a heavy 10- to 12-inch skillet, melt the 3 tablespoons of butter and 3 tablespoons of oil over moderate heat. When the foam subsides, carefully slide in the *bastila* and fry it for 2 or 3 minutes, or until the bottom is golden brown. With the aid of a wide spatula, slide the *bastila* onto a plate. Place a second plate upside down over the *bastila* and, grasping both plates firmly together, invert them. Slide the *bastila* back into the skillet and brown the other side for 2 or 3 minutes.

Transfer the *bastila* to a heated platter and sprinkle it with the sugar-and-cinnamon mixture. Cut it into wedges and serve at once.

Meat

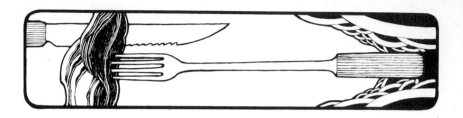

Musaca cu Cartofi *(Romania)*
GROUND-VEAL CASSEROLE WITH POTATOES

To serve 6

6 tablespoons butter, softened
2 tablespoons soft fresh crumbs,
 made from homemade-type white
 bread, pulverized in a blender or
 finely shredded with a fork
8 medium-sized boiling potatoes
 (about 2½ pounds)
1 cup finely chopped onions
1 pound lean ground veal
2 tablespoons flour
¼ cup dry white wine

¼ cup finely chopped fresh parsley
2 tablespoons finely cut fresh fennel
 leaves, or substitute ½ teaspoon
 powdered fennel
¼ teaspoon crumbled dried thyme
1 teaspoon salt
½ teaspoon freshly ground black
 pepper
2 egg yolks, lightly beaten, plus 2 eggs
2 tablespoons butter, cut into
 ¼-inch bits
1 cup heavy cream

With a pastry brush, spread 2 tablespoons of the softened butter over the bottom and sides of a 2-quart casserole 3 inches deep. Add the bread crumbs and tip the casserole from side to side to spread them evenly. Set aside. With a small, sharp knife or swivel-bladed vegetable parer, peel the potatoes, dropping them into cold water as you proceed. Then, cut the potatoes into ¼-inch-thick slices and return them to the water.

In a heavy 10- to 12-inch skillet, heat 2 tablespoons of butter over moderate heat. When the foam begins to subside, pat a handful of potatoes completely dry with paper towels and drop them into the skillet. Turning them frequently with a spatula, fry the potatoes for 4 or 5 minutes, until they are golden brown on both sides. As they brown, transfer the slices to paper towels to drain while you dry and fry the remaining potatoes, adding more butter to the skillet when necessary.

When the potatoes are browned, add 2 more tablespoons of butter to the skillet and drop in the onions. Stirring frequently, cook for about 5 minutes, or until they are soft and translucent but not brown. Add the veal and, mashing it frequently with the back of a spoon to break up any lumps, cook until no trace of pink remains.

Stir in the flour and cook for a minute or two, then remove from the heat and beat in the wine, parsley, fennel, thyme, salt and pepper. Let the mixture cool for about 5 minutes and stir in the egg yolks one at a time, stirring until no trace of yolk is visible. Taste for seasoning.

Preheat the oven to 400°. Assemble the *musaca cu cartofi* in the following fashion: Spread about one third of the potato slices on the bottom of the casserole, overlapping them neatly. Spread half the meat mixture evenly over the potatoes, add another layer of potato slices, and then add the rest of the meat, spreading it out as before. Cover with the remaining potato slices and scatter the 2 tablespoons of butter bits on top.

Bake covered in the middle of the oven for 30 minutes. Then beat the 2 eggs and the cream together with a whisk or a rotary beater and pour evenly over the *musaca*. Bake uncovered for 30 minutes longer, or until the top is golden brown. Serve at once, directly from the casserole.

Émincé de Veau *(Switzerland)*
VEAL STRIPS IN WHITE WINE AND CREAM SAUCE

To serve 4

5 tablespoons butter
3 tablespoons vegetable oil
1½ pounds veal scallops, sliced
    ¼ inch thick and cut into strips
    about 2 inches long and ¼ inch wide
1 tablespoon finely chopped shallots,

or substitute 1 tablespoon
    finely chopped scallions,
    using only the white parts
⅓ cup Neuchâtel, Fendant or other
    dry white wine
1 cup heavy cream
Salt
White pepper

In a heavy 10- to 12-inch skillet, melt 2 tablespoons of the butter with the oil over high heat. When the foam subsides, drop in half the veal and, tossing the strips about constantly with a fork, fry for about 2 minutes. When the veal is delicately colored, transfer it to a large sieve set over a bowl. Melt 2 more tablespoons of butter in the pan, then drop in the remaining veal and cook as before. Add the veal and its juices to the veal in the sieve. Add the remaining butter to the pan and melt it over moderate heat. Then stir in the shallots and cook for about 2 minutes before pouring in the wine. Raise the heat to high and stir until the liquid comes to a boil. Immediately add the cream and all the drained veal juices. Stirring constantly, boil briskly for 8 to 10 minutes, or until the sauce has reduced to about half its original volume and thickened lightly. Taste for seasoning. Return the veal to the skillet and turn it about until it is thoroughly coated with the sauce. Simmer over low heat for 2 or 3 minutes until the veal is heated through. Serve at once, accompanied, if you like, by *Rösti (page 95)*.

Veau Cordon Bleu *(Switzerland)*

BREADED VEAL SCALLOPS

To serve 4

Four 6-by-4-inch veal scallops
(about 4 ounces each), cut about
⅜ inch thick and pounded ¼
inch thick
2 eggs, lightly beaten with 2
tablespoons milk
½ cup flour
¼ pound imported Swiss Gruyère
cheese, cut into 4 strips, each 3
inches long, 1 inch wide and ¼
inch thick
4 slices boiled ham, each 3 inches
square and ⅛ inch thick
1 cup fine dry bread crumbs
4 tablespoons butter
1 cup vegetable oil
4 thin lemon slices
Paprika

With a pastry brush, coat one side of each veal scallop lightly with the egg-and-milk mixture and sprinkle with a light dusting of the flour. Wrap each strip of cheese in a slice of ham and place it lengthwise in the center of the coated side of a scallop. Fold the scallop in half lengthwise to make a 6-inch-long packet enclosing the ham and cheese completely, and press the edges firmly together to seal them tightly. One at a time, coat the scallops with the remaining flour and shake them free of any excess. Then dip them first in the remaining egg-and-milk mixture and then in the bread crumbs, making sure each scallop is thoroughly coated with crumbs. Set the scallops side by side on a plate or wax paper and refrigerate for at least 1 hour.

In a heavy 12-inch skillet, melt the butter with the oil over moderate heat until the foam subsides and the fat colors lightly. Add the scallops, turning them occasionally with tongs or a slotted spoon, and fry for 15 to 20 minutes, or until they are golden brown and crisp on both sides. Drain on paper towels and serve at once from a heated platter. Top each scallop with a slice of lemon sprinkled lightly with paprika.

Suri Läberli und Nierli *(Switzerland)*

LIVER AND KIDNEYS IN RED WINE

To serve 4

3 tablespoons butter
2 tablespoons finely chopped onions
⅓ cup dry red wine
1 teaspoon red wine vinegar
1 veal kidney (about 1 pound),
peeled, trimmed of fat, and cut
into ½-inch cubes
½ pound calf's liver, trimmed and
cut into ½-inch squares
½ teaspoon salt
1 tablespoon finely chopped fresh
parsley

In a small skillet, melt 1 tablespoon of the butter over moderate heat. Add the onions and, stirring frequently, cook for about 5 minutes, or until they are soft and transparent but not brown. Watch carefully for any sign of burning and regulate the heat accordingly. Pour in the wine and wine vinegar and, stirring constantly, bring to a boil over high heat. Cook briskly, uncovered, until the liquid is thick and syrupy. Remove the pan from the heat.

Immediately melt the remaining 2 tablespoons of butter over high heat in a heavy 10- to 12-inch skillet. When the foam begins to subside, add the kidneys and liver. Turning the pieces of meat about constantly with a spoon, sauté for 2 to 3 minutes, until they are lightly and evenly browned. Stir in the reserved sauce and, still stirring, cook for 60 seconds longer. Add the salt, taste for seasoning, and transfer the entire contents of the skillet to a heated platter. Sprinkle the kidneys and liver with the parsley and serve at once.

Teloshko s Khrian *(Bulgaria)*
VEAL STEW WITH HORSERADISH

To serve 4

2 pounds boneless veal shoulder, trimmed of excess fat and cut into 1-inch cubes
3 cups chicken stock, fresh or canned
3 cups cold water
2 teaspoons salt
Freshly ground black pepper
3 medium-sized carrots, scraped and cut into ½-inch dice (about 2 cups)
3 medium-sized celery stalks, trimmed of all leaves and cut into ½-inch dice (about 2 cups)
2 medium-sized boiling potatoes, peeled and cut into ½-inch dice (about 2 cups)
2 tablespoons freshly grated horseradish, or substitute 4 ounces prepared white horseradish, squeezed dry in a towel
2 teaspoons white distilled vinegar

In a heavy 3- to 4-quart casserole, combine the veal, chicken stock, water, salt and a few grindings of pepper. Bring to a boil over high heat, skimming off the scum and foam as they rise to the surface. Reduce the heat to low, partially cover the casserole, and simmer for 30 minutes. Stir in the carrots, celery and potatoes, and simmer partially covered for about 20 minutes longer, or until the meat is tender and the vegetables are soft but still intact. Stir in the horseradish and vinegar, and taste for seasoning; if you have used prepared horseradish, add more vinegar to taste if you want. Serve at once, directly from the casserole or from a heated bowl.

Zürcher Leberspiessli *(Switzerland)*
SKEWERED CALF'S LIVER AND BACON

To serve 4

1½ pounds fresh spinach, or	into halves
substitute two 10-ounce packages	7 tablespoons butter
frozen chopped spinach,	¼ cup vegetable oil
thoroughly defrosted	2 tablespoons finely chopped onions
20 dried sage leaves	¼ teaspoon finely chopped garlic
1½ pounds calf's liver, sliced ¾	½ teaspoon salt
inch thick, then cut in 1-inch	Freshly ground black pepper
squares	¼ cup Neuchâtel or other dry
10 lean bacon slices, cut crosswise	white wine

Wash the fresh spinach under cold running water. Drain, then strip the leaves from the stems and discard the stems and any discolored leaves. In a heavy 2- to 3-quart saucepan, bring ½ cup of water to a boil. Add the spinach, lower the heat, and simmer tightly covered for about 3 minutes. Drain the spinach in a sieve, cool, and squeeze it completely dry. Chop it as fine as possible. (Frozen spinach needs only to be drained, squeezed dry, then finely chopped.) Set the spinach aside.

Press a small sage leaf on each piece of liver and wrap each piece of liver in a strip of bacon. Thread 5 squares of liver apiece on four 6- to 8-inch-long thin metal skewers, pressing the pieces tightly together. In a heavy 12-inch skillet, melt 3 tablespoons of the butter with the oil over moderate heat. When the fat begins to color very lightly, arrange the skewers side by side in the skillet. Fry uncovered, turning the skewers occasionally, for 10 to 15 minutes, or until the bacon is brown and crisp. Regulate the heat if necessary to prevent the bacon from burning.

Meanwhile, in a heavy 8- to 10-inch skillet, melt the remaining butter over moderate heat. When the foam subsides, add the onions and garlic and, stirring frequently, cook for 2 or 3 minutes, until they are soft and transparent. Drop in the spinach, add the salt and a few grindings of pepper, and stir for a few minutes longer, until the ingredients are thoroughly combined and the spinach is heated through.

Spread the spinach on a heated platter and arrange the skewers of liver side by side on top. Then, working quickly, discard the fat remaining in the skillet in which the liver was fried. Pour in the wine and bring to a boil over high heat, stirring constantly and scraping in the brown particles clinging to the bottom and sides of the pan. Let the sauce boil for a moment or so, then pour it evenly over the liver and serve at once.

Lamstongen met Rozijnensaus *(Netherlands)*
LAMBS' TONGUES WITH RAISIN SAUCE

To serve 6 to 8

12 fresh lambs' tongues, 6 to 8 ounces each	1½ teaspoons salt
2 medium-sized onions, peeled	½ cup light-brown sugar
2 garlic cloves, peeled and crushed with the side of a cleaver or heavy knife	½ cup seedless raisins
	¼ teaspoon ground cumin
	¼ teaspoon powdered marjoram
1 large bay leaf	½ cup dry white wine
	2 tablespoons cornstarch

In a heavy 4- to 5-quart casserole, combine the lambs' tongues, onions, garlic, bay leaf and 1 teaspoon of the salt. Pour in enough cold water to cover the tongues by about 1 inch and bring to a boil over high heat, meanwhile skimming off any scum and foam that rise to the surface. Reduce the heat to low, cover partially, and simmer for about 2 hours, or until the tongues are tender and show no resistance when pierced with the point of a small, sharp knife.

Transfer the tongues to a cutting board and let them cool slightly. Strain the stock remaining in the casserole through a fine sieve set over a bowl, pressing down hard on the onions and garlic with the back of a spoon to extract all their juices before discarding them. Pour 2 cups of the stock into a heavy 12-inch skillet, leaving the rest in the bowl. While the tongues are still somewhat warm, skin them with a small, sharp knife and cut away the fat, bones and gristle at the base of each one. Carve the tongues crosswise into ⅓-inch-thick slices and set the slices aside in the bowl of stock to keep them moist.

Stir the brown sugar, raisins, cumin, marjoram and remaining ½ teaspoon of salt into the 2 cups of stock in the skillet. Bring to a boil over high heat, stirring until the sugar dissolves completely. Reduce the heat to a simmer. Make a smooth paste of the wine and cornstarch and, stirring constantly, pour it in a slow thin stream into the simmering raisin sauce. Still stirring, simmer until the sauce thickens heavily and comes to a boil. If it seems too thick for your taste, thin it with as much of the reserved stock as you like. With a slotted spoon, transfer the tongue slices to the skillet. Turn them about to coat them evenly with the sauce, then reduce the heat to the lowest possible point and simmer partially covered for about 10 minutes, or until the tongue is heated through. Taste for seasoning and serve at once from a deep heated platter. *Lamstongen met rozijnensaus* is usually accompanied by hot boiled rice.

Rognons de Veau à la Liégeoise *(Belgium)*
SAUTÉED VEAL KIDNEYS WITH JUNIPER BERRIES

To serve 4

4 veal kidneys (about 6 to 8 ounces each), peeled and trimmed of excess fat
Salt
Freshly ground black pepper
4 tablespoons butter

2 tablespoons vegetable oil
16 juniper berries, slightly bruised with the flat of a cleaver or large, heavy knife
½ cup gin
¼ cup chicken stock, fresh or canned
1 tablespoon butter, softened

With a sharp knife cut through each kidney horizontally to within about ½ inch of the rounded edge. Open the kidneys gently and spread them as flat as possible. Then, to hold them in shape, thread 2 short metal skewers diagonally crosswise to one another through each kidney *(see drawing below)*. Sprinkle the kidneys on both sides with a little salt and a few grindings of pepper.

In a heavy 12-inch skillet, melt the 4 tablespoons of butter with the oil over high heat. When the foam begins to subside, drop in the juniper berries and place the kidneys in the pan cut side down. Sauté the kidneys for 4 to 5 minutes on each side, or until they are lightly browned.

Warm the gin in a small pan over low heat, ignite it with a match, and pour it flaming over the kidneys, meanwhile sliding the skillet back and forth over the heat. When the flames die, transfer the kidneys with tongs or a slotted spatula to a heated platter and drape the platter with foil to keep the kidneys warm while you make the sauce.

Add the chicken stock to the liquid remaining in the skillet and bring to a boil over high heat, meanwhile scraping in any brown particles that cling to the bottom and sides of the pan. Cook briskly, uncovered, until the sauce is reduced to a syrupy glaze. Remove the pan from the heat and swirl in the tablespoon of softened butter. Carefully remove the skewers from the kidneys, pour the sauce over them, and serve at once, accompanied perhaps by *pommes à la liégeoise (Recipe Index)*.

Market Khastel *(Tunisia)*
LAMB WITH CHESTNUTS AND RAISINS

To serve 4

12 fresh chestnuts
2¼ cups water
1½ pounds lean boneless lamb
   shoulder, trimmed of excess fat
   and cut into 1½-inch chunks

¼ teaspoon ground cinnamon
1 teaspoon salt
¼ teaspoon freshly ground black
   pepper
½ cup vegetable oil
1 cup seedless raisins
1 teaspoon sugar

Preheat the oven to 425°. With a small, sharp knife, cut a deep crisscross into the top of each chestnut. Arrange the chestnuts in a single layer in a shallow baking pan, and pour in about ¼ cup of water—just enough to film the bottom. Roast the chestnuts in the middle of the oven for about 10 minutes, or until they pop open. Turn off the oven and remove half the nuts from the pan. While they are still hot, remove their shells and inner brown membranes with a small, sharp knife. Then peel the remaining hot chestnuts similarly.

Pat the chunks of lamb completely dry with paper towels and drop them into a bowl. Add the cinnamon, salt and pepper, and toss the meat about with a wooden spoon to season the pieces evenly. In a heavy 10- to 12-inch skillet, heat the oil over high heat until a light haze forms above it. Brown the lamb in the hot oil, turning the chunks frequently with a slotted spoon or spatula and regulating the heat so they color richly and evenly on all sides without burning. Add the chestnuts and remaining 2 cups of water and bring to a boil. Reduce the heat to low and simmer partially covered for 30 minutes.

Stir in the raisins and sugar, partially cover the skillet again, and simmer for 20 to 30 minutes longer, or until the lamb is tender and shows no resistance when pierced deeply with the point of a small, sharp knife. Taste for seasoning, then serve at once from a heated platter or bowl.

Tajine Qamama *(Morocco)*
LAMB, ONION AND HONEY CASSEROLE

To serve 6

3 pounds lean boneless lamb
    shoulder, trimmed of excess fat
    and cut into 1-inch pieces
1 teaspoon crumbled saffron threads
    or ground saffron
1 teaspoon ground cinnamon

½ teaspoon ground ginger
3 cups cold water
4 tablespoons honey
2 pounds white onions, each about
    1 inch in diameter, trimmed and
    peeled

Preheat the oven to 350°. In a heavy 4- to 5-quart casserole, combine the lamb, saffron, cinnamon, ginger, water and 2 tablespoons of the honey. The liquid should cover the lamb halfway; add more water if necessary. Bring to a boil over high heat, stirring occasionally. Then reduce the heat to low and simmer partially covered for 30 to 35 minutes. Remove the casserole from the heat and drain the liquid into a small saucepan. Boil it briskly, uncovered, over the high heat until it is reduced to 2 cups. Pour the reduced liquid back into the casserole and add the onions and the remaining 2 tablespoons of honey. Stir until all the ingredients are well mixed, partially cover, and bake in the middle of the oven for about 30 minutes, or until the lamb and onions are brown and tender and the liquid has almost evaporated. Serve at once from a heated platter or deep bowl.

El Lahm el M'qali *(Morocco)*
LAMB WITH LEMONS AND OLIVES

To serve 4

½ cup olive oil
A pinch of ground ginger
¼ teaspoon pulverized saffron
    threads or ground saffron
1½ teaspoons salt
2 pounds boneless lamb shoulder,
    trimmed of excess fat and cut into
    1-inch cubes

2 cups finely chopped onions
¼ teaspoon finely chopped garlic
6 sprigs fresh coriander *(cilantro)*
2 salted lemons *(page 99),*
    separated into quarters, or 2 fresh
    lemons, cut lengthwise into
    quarters and seeded
16 small green olives

In a heavy 12-inch sauté pan stir the olive oil, ginger, saffron and salt together. Add the lamb and turn the pieces about to coat them evenly. Pour in 3 cups of water, then add the onions, garlic, coriander and lemons.

The liquid should almost cover the lamb; if necessary, add up to one more cup of water. Bring to a boil over high heat, then reduce the heat to low, cover tightly, and simmer for about 1 hour, or until the lamb is tender and shows no resistance when pierced with the point of a small knife. With a slotted spoon, transfer the lamb to a plate.

Bring the sauce remaining in the pan to a boil over high heat and cook briskly, uncovered, until it thickens slightly and is reduced to about 3 cups. Discard the coriander. Return the lamb and the liquid that has accumulated around it to the pan, add the olives and, stirring frequently, simmer for 4 to 5 minutes, until heated through. Taste for seasoning. Transfer the contents of the skillet to a heated bowl and serve at once.

Lahm Lhalou *(Algeria)*

LAMB AND PRUNES WITH ALMONDS ("SWEET MEAT")

To serve 6

2½ pounds boneless lamb
   shoulder, trimmed of excess fat
   and cut into 1½-inch cubes
½ teaspoon salt
2 tablespoons unsalted butter
1 cup water

1 cinnamon stick, broken into
   1-inch lengths
1 cup whole blanched almonds
1 cup sugar
2 tablespoons orange-blossom water
   (see Glossary)
¾ pound pitted prunes

Pat the lamb dry with paper towels and sprinkle on all sides with the salt. In a heavy 3- to 4-quart casserole, melt the butter over moderate heat. When the foam subsides, add about half of the lamb and brown it in the hot fat, turning the cubes frequently with tongs or a slotted spatula. As they brown, transfer the cubes to a plate and brown the remaining lamb similarly. Add the water, cinnamon, almonds, sugar and orange-blossom water to the fat remaining in the casserole and, stirring constantly, bring to a boil over high heat. Return the lamb and the liquid that has accumulated around it to the casserole, reduce the heat to low and simmer covered for 45 minutes. Then add the prunes and turn them about to coat them with the cooking liquid. Simmer covered for 10 minutes longer, or until the lamb shows no resistance when pierced with a small knife.

Serve at once, mounded on a heated platter. Because this is an exceedingly rich dish, the Algerians never serve it as a main course but rather as one of the dishes in a multiple-course meal. It often precedes or follows chicken *couscous* *(page 42)*.

Musaca cu Tatei *(Romania)*
GROUND-PORK CASSEROLE WITH NOODLES AND CHEESE

To serve 6

4 tablespoons butter, softened
2 slices homemade-type white bread
   with crusts removed, cut ½ inch
   thick and torn into small pieces
½ cup milk
2 tablespoons salt
1 pound fine egg noodles
6 eggs
2 pounds lean ground pork
2 tablespoons finely chopped leeks,
   white part only, thoroughly
   washed to rid them of all sand

2 tablespoons finely chopped fresh
   parsley
2 tablespoons finely cut fresh fennel
   leaves or ¼ teaspoon powdered
   fennel
Freshly ground black pepper
6 tablespoons butter, cut into
   ¼-inch bits
½ cup heavy cream
¼ cup finely grated Kashkaval
   cheese, or substitute sweet
   Münster or Provolone

Preheat the oven to 400°. With a pastry brush, spread the softened butter evenly over the bottom and sides of a heavy 3-quart casserole. Combine the bread bits and milk in a bowl and set aside.

Bring 4 quarts of water to a boil in a 6- to 8-quart pot. Add 1 tablespoon salt, drop in the noodles, and stir with a fork to prevent the strands from sticking to one another or to the bottom and sides of the pot. Stirring occasionally, boil briskly, uncovered, for 6 to 8 minutes, or until the noodles are tender but still slightly resistant to the bite. Drain the noodles in a large colander, lifting the strands with two forks to make certain all the water drains off. Then, in a deep bowl, beat 4 of the eggs and 2 teaspoons of salt with a whisk or a rotary beater for 1 to 2 minutes. Add the noodles and turn them about with a fork until they are evenly coated. Set aside.

Meanwhile, combine the pork, the bread and milk, the leeks, parsley, fennel, 1 teaspoon of salt and a few grindings of pepper in a large bowl. Knead vigorously with both hands, then beat with a wooden spoon until the mixture is smooth and fluffy.

To assemble the *musaca,* spread about one third of the noodles evenly in the bottom of the buttered casserole. Spoon half of the meat mixture over the noodles, smoothing the top with a spatula. Sprinkle with 2 tablespoons of the butter bits, then add one half of the remaining noodles. Cover the noodles with the rest of the meat mixture, scatter 2 tablespoons of butter bits over it, and add the remaining noodles. Top with the rest of the butter bits, then cover the casserole with its lid.

Bake in the middle of the oven for 30 minutes. Beat the remaining 2 eggs, the heavy cream and grated cheese together with a whisk or fork, and when they are well mixed pour them evenly over the *musaca.* Cover again and bake for 1 hour longer, removing the cover for the final 30 minutes to allow the top to brown.

To unmold and serve the *musaca,* run a thin knife all around the sides of the casserole. Place an inverted serving plate over the top and, grasping plate and casserole together firmly, carefully turn them over. The *musaca* should slide out easily. Serve at once.

Qodban *(Morocco)*
MARINATED LAMB KABOBS

To serve 4

¼ cup strained fresh lemon juice
½ cup olive oil
2 tablespoons finely chopped fresh coriander *(cilantro)*
1 tablespoon finely chopped garlic
2 tablespoons finely chopped fresh parsley
1 teaspoon ground ginger

1 teaspoon turmeric
½ teaspoon ground cumin
1 teaspoon salt
2 pounds lean boneless lamb, preferably from the leg, trimmed of excess fat and cut into 1-inch cubes
3 pounds fresh beef suet, cut into 1-inch cubes

Combine the lemon juice, olive oil, coriander, garlic, parsley, ginger, turmeric, cumin and salt in a deep bowl and stir until all the ingredients are mixed. Drop in the lamb and turn the pieces about with a spoon to coat them well. Marinate at room temperature for at least 2 hours, or in the refrigerator for 6 hours, turning the lamb occasionally.

Light a layer of coals in a charcoal broiler and let them burn until a white ash appears on the surface, or preheat the broiler of your range to its highest point.

Remove the cubes of lamb and discard the marinade. Then, starting with a cube of suet and ending with one of lamb, thread the suet and lamb cubes alternately on six long skewers, pressing the suet and lamb firmly together.

Broil 4 inches from the heat, turning the skewers occasionally, until the lamb is done to your taste. For pink lamb, allow about 10 minutes; for the more traditionally Moroccan well-done lamb, broil the *qodban* for about 15 minutes.

Slide the lamb off the skewers onto a heated platter and discard the fat. *Qodban* will serve two or three as a main course or four as one of the dishes for a traditional Moroccan meal of many courses.

Zrazy *(Poland)*
BEEF ROLLS WITH SOUR-CREAM SAUCE

To serve 4

1 teaspoon salt

5 tablespoons unsalted butter
3 tablespoons vegetable oil
3 cups finely chopped onions
1½ pounds fresh mushrooms,
 including the stems, finely
 chopped (6 cups)
¼ cup soft fresh crumbs made
 from homemade-type white
 bread, pulverized in a blender or
 finely shredded with a fork

2 pounds top round steak, sliced
 ½ inch thick, trimmed of
 excess fat and pounded ¼ inch
 thick
Freshly ground black pepper
3 tablespoons flour
1 cup fresh beef stock, or ½ cup
 canned condensed beef stock
 combined with ½ cup cold water
⅔ cup sour cream

Preheat the oven to 350°. In a heavy 12-inch skillet, melt 2 tablespoons of the butter and 1 tablespoon of the oil over moderate heat. When the foam begins to subside, add the onions and mushrooms and, stirring frequently, cook for 8 to 10 minutes, or until the liquid that has begun to accumulate in the pan has evaporated. Do not let the mushrooms brown. Stir in the bread crumbs and ½ teaspoon of the salt, and remove the pan from the heat. Taste for seasoning.

Cut the round steak into 8 rectangular pieces about 3 or 4 inches wide and 6 to 8 inches long. Sprinkle the steaks evenly on both sides with the remaining salt and a few grindings of pepper. Divide the mushroom mixture into eight equal portions and place one portion at the shorter end of each steak. Then roll the steaks into cylinders enclosing the filling, tucking in the sides. Tie the rolls at each end with kitchen cord.

Roll the *zrazy* in the flour and shake them vigorously to remove any excess. In the 12-inch skillet, melt the remaining butter and oil over high heat. Brown the rolls in the hot fat, turning them about frequently with tongs or a metal spatula and regulating the heat so they color richly and evenly without burning. As they brown transfer the rolls to a heavy casserole large enough to hold them in one layer.

Pour off all but a thin film of fat from the skillet and in its place add the beef stock or stock and water. Bring to a boil over high heat, stirring constantly and scraping in any brown particles that cling to the bottom and sides of the pan. Pour the liquid over the rolls and cover the casserole tightly. Braise in the middle of the oven for 45 minutes, or until the beef is tender and shows no resistance when pierced deeply with the point of a small skewer or knife. Transfer the rolls to a heated platter, cut off the strings, and cover the rolls with foil to keep them warm while you make the sauce.

With a large spoon, skim off and discard as much fat as possible from the liquid remaining in the casserole. Stirring constantly, bring the liquid to a boil over high heat. Remove from the heat and stir in the sour cream.

Taste for seasoning, pour over the beef and serve at once. *Zrazy* is traditionally accompanied by boiled rice or *kasha* (buckwheat groats).

Tajin Gannariya (Tunisia)
LAMB, CHEESE AND ARTICHOKE CASSEROLE

To serve 6 to 8

1 quart water	12 artichoke hearts, thoroughly
¼ cup dried white, pea or Great	defrosted if frozen
Northern beans	½ cup soft fresh crumbs made
1 pound lean boneless lamb	from homemade-type white
shoulder, trimmed of excess fat	bread, pulverized in a blender or
and cut into ½-inch cubes	finely shredded with a fork
1 teaspoon salt	¼ cup freshly grated imported
¼ teaspoon freshly ground black	Parmesan cheese
pepper	⅛ teaspoon crumbled saffron
⅓ cup olive oil	threads or ground saffron
½ cup finely chopped onions	2 tablespoons butter, melted
2 tablespoons canned tomato purée	6 eggs, lightly beaten

Bring 1 quart of water to a boil in a 2- to 3-quart saucepan. Drop in the dried beans and boil briskly for 2 minutes. Then turn off the heat and let the beans soak for 1 hour. Bring the beans to a boil again over high heat, reduce the heat to low, and simmer partially covered for 30 minutes.

Meanwhile, pat the cubes of lamb completely dry with paper towels and sprinkle the meat with the salt and pepper. In a heavy 12-inch skillet, warm the oil over moderate heat. Add the lamb and onions and, stirring frequently, cook for 6 to 8 minutes, until the lamb is brown on all sides. Watch carefully for any sign of burning and regulate the heat accordingly. Stir in the beans, the bean liquid and the tomato purée, and bring to a boil. Reduce the heat to low and simmer partially covered for 1 hour, until the beans are tender but still intact. Remove from the heat.

Ladle about 1 cup of the cooking liquid into a fine sieve set over a small saucepan and set the strained sauce aside. Transfer the remaining contents of the skillet to a bowl and cool to room temperature.

Preheat the oven to 350°. Add the artichoke hearts, bread crumbs, cheese, saffron and 1 tablespoon of the melted butter to the lamb mixture and toss gently but thoroughly together. Taste for seasoning, then stir in the beaten eggs. Pour the mixture into a 2-quart soufflé or baking dish and bake in the middle of the oven for about 35 minutes. The *tajin gannariya* is done when the top is golden brown and a knife inserted in the center comes out clean.

Just before serving, directly from the baking dish, pour the remaining tablespoon of melted butter over the *tajin*. Reheat the reserved sauce briefly and present it separately in a bowl or sauceboat.

Kiełbasa *(Poland)*
GARLIC-FLAVORED PORK SAUSAGE

To make 3 sausages, each about 30
  inches long

4 pounds boneless pork shoulder,
  cut into 1-inch pieces
1 pound beef shin, cut into 1-inch
  pieces
2 tablespoons plus ½ teaspoon salt

3 three-foot lengths of hog sausage
  casing
½ teaspoon freshly ground black
  pepper
4 cloves garlic, finely chopped
¼ teaspoon curing saltpeter *(see
  Glossary)*

Place the pork in one bowl and the beef shin in another and sprinkle each with 1 tablespoon of salt. Toss to distribute the salt evenly and set aside in a cool, not cold, place for 24 hours.

Place the sausage casing in a bowl, pour in enough warm water to cover it by 1 inch, and soak 2 or 3 hours, until it is soft and pliable.

Put the pieces of pork once through the coarsest blade of a meat grinder, then put the beef through the finest blade 4 times. In a deep bowl, combine the ground meats with the remaining ½ teaspoon of salt, the pepper, garlic and saltpeter. Knead the mixture vigorously with both hands, then beat with a wooden spoon until smooth and fluffy.

Wash the sausage casing thoroughly but gently under cold, slowly running water to remove all traces of the salt in which it was preserved. Hold one end securely around the faucet and let the cold water run through to rinse the inside of the casing. To make each sausage, tie a knot about 3 inches from the end of one length of casing. Fit the open end snugly over the funnel (or "horn") on the sausage-making attachment of a meat grinder. Then ease the rest of the casing up onto the funnel, squeezing it together like the folds of an accordion. Spoon the meat mix-

To make sausage by hand, tie a knot about 3 inches from one end of a cleaned sausage casing and fit the open end over the spout of a wide-based funnel, easing most of the casing up onto the spout. Then spoon the meat mixture into the funnel and push it through into the casing with your fingers. Knot the open end and roll the sausage gently on a firm surface to distribute the filling evenly.

ture into the mouth of the funnel and with a wooden pestle push it through into the casing. As you fill it, the casing will expand and gradually ease away from the funnel in a coil. Fill the casing to within an inch or so of the open end; do not stuff it too tight or it may burst. Slip the casing off the funnel and knot the open end. You may cook the sausages immediately or refrigerate them safely for 5 or 6 days.

Before cooking, prick the casing in 5 or 6 places with the point of a skewer or a small knife. Coil the sausages in concentric circles in a heavy 10- to 12-inch skillet and pour in enough water to cover them completely. Bring to a simmer over moderate heat, then simmer uncovered for about 40 minutes. *Kiełbasa* is traditionally sliced into rounds ½ inch thick, fried in a little vegetable oil until no trace of pink shows in the meat, and served with sauerkraut and boiled potatoes. It may also be served cold, or used in *bigos* and *erwtensoep (Recipe Index)*.

If you do not have a meat grinder, ask the butcher to grind the pork coarsely and the beef very fine. Following the recipe, combine the meats with the seasonings, and fill the sausages as illustrated opposite.

Pieczony Schab (Poland)
ROAST LOIN OF PORK WITH APPLESAUCE GLAZE

To serve 6 to 8

	in 4 or 5 places with kitchen cord
A 5- to 5½-pound pork loin in one piece, with the backbone sawed through lengthwise but left attached and tied to the loin	1 teaspoon salt
	Freshly ground black pepper
	8 whole cloves
	1 cup thick applesauce

Preheat the oven to 350°. Rub the pork loin on all sides with the salt and a liberal grinding of pepper. Stud the loin with the cloves, spacing them along its length as evenly as possible.

Place the pork loin fat side up in a shallow roasting pan just large enough to hold it comfortably. For the most predictable roasting results, insert the tip of a meat thermometer horizontally at least 2 inches into one side of the loin. Be sure the tip of the meat thermometer does not touch any fat or bone.

Roast the loin undisturbed in the middle of the oven for 1 hour. Remove the pan from the oven and, with a spatula, spread the applesauce evenly over the top of the loin. Roast for about 30 minutes longer, or until the applesauce has become a golden brown glaze and the meat thermometer indicates a temperature of 160° to 165°.

Transfer the roast pork to a heated platter and let it rest for about 10 minutes for easier carving. Traditionally, the roast pork is accompanied by pickled plums and sauerkraut-and-apple salad *(Recipe Index)*.

Mititei *(Romania)*
GRILLED BEEF SAUSAGES

To make about 18 small sausages

2 pounds lean ground beef,
   preferably neck, ground together
   with ¼ pound fresh beef kidney
   suet
2 teaspoons finely chopped garlic
½ teaspoon ground allspice

¼ teaspoon ground cloves
¼ teaspoon crumbled dried thyme
1½ teaspoons salt
⅛ teaspoon freshly ground black
   pepper
½ cup beef stock, fresh or canned
Vegetable oil

Combine the beef and suet with the garlic, allspice, cloves, thyme, salt and pepper in a deep bowl. Knead vigorously with both hands until the ingredients are well blended. Then pour in the stock and beat with a wooden spoon until the mixture is smooth and fluffy. Taste for seasoning.

Divide the mixture into 18 equal portions and roll each one into a cylinder about 3½ inches long and 1 inch thick, moistening your hands with cold water as you proceed.

Preheat the broiler to its highest setting. Brush the rack of a broiler pan lightly with oil and arrange the sausages side by side on the rack. Broil them about 3 inches from the heat for about 8 minutes, turning them with a spatula or tongs every few minutes until they are crisp and brown on all sides.

Serve the *mititei* at once from a heated platter. Traditionally, the sausages are accompanied by peppers in oil *(page 86)* and sour dill pickles.

Gevulde Pannekoek *(Netherlands)*
MEAT-FILLED PANCAKE

To serve 4

BATTER
1 cup all-purpose flour
2 eggs

1½ cups milk
½ teaspoon salt

Combine the 1 cup of flour, eggs, milk and ½ teaspoon of salt in the jar of an electric blender and blend at high speed for 30 seconds. Turn off the machine, scrape down the sides of the jar with a rubber spatula, and blend again for about 15 seconds, or until the pancake batter is smooth. To make the batter by hand, stir the flour and eggs together in a mixing bowl and gradually stir in the milk and salt. Beat with a wire whisk or a rotary or electric beater until the batter is smooth. In either case, set the batter aside at room temperature to rest for about 30 minutes before using it.

FILLING

4 tablespoons butter	canned
2 tablespoons finely chopped onions	2 teaspoons strained fresh lemon
1 cup finely chopped fresh	juice
mushrooms (about ¼ pound)	¼ teaspoon ground nutmeg
1 pound lean ground beef	1 teaspoon salt
⅓ cup flour	Freshly ground black pepper
2 cups chicken stock, fresh or	2 teaspoons melted butter

Meanwhile, in a heavy 8- to 10-inch skillet, melt 2 tablespoons of butter over moderate heat. When the foam begins to subside, add the onions and, stirring frequently, cook for 1 or 2 minutes, until they are soft but not brown. Drop in the mushrooms and, stirring frequently, cook for 10 to 15 minutes, or until most of the liquid in the pan has evaporated. Lower the heat if necessary to prevent the mushrooms from browning. Add the beef and, mashing frequently with the back of a spoon to break up any lumps, cook until all traces of pink disappear. Scrape the entire contents of the pan into a sieve set over a bowl and drain. Discard any liquid that accumulates in the bowl.

In a separate 8- to 10-inch skillet, melt the remaining 2 tablespoons of butter over moderate heat. With a wooden spoon, stir in the ⅓ cup of flour and mix thoroughly. Pour in the chicken stock and, stirring constantly with a whisk, cook over high heat until the sauce comes to a boil and thickens heavily. Reduce the heat to low and simmer for about 5 minutes, then whisk in the lemon juice, nutmeg, 1 teaspoon of salt and a few grindings of black pepper. Remove the skillet from the heat, stir in the drained meat mixture, and taste for seasoning. Cover loosely with foil to keep warm.

Just before serving, heat an 8-inch skillet over moderate heat until a drop of water flicked into it steams for 2 seconds before it evaporates. Brush the pan with 1 teaspoon of the melted butter and immediately pour in half the pancake batter, tipping the pan gently from side to side so that the batter covers the bottom evenly. Cook for 3 or 4 minutes, until the top of the pancake is dry and the bottom is golden brown. Loosen the side of the pancake with a metal spatula and carefully slide it out of the pan onto a heated serving platter, "uncooked" side up. Quickly brush the pan again with the remaining melted butter, pour in the rest of the batter and make a second pancake in the same manner. When the bottom is brown, loosen it with the spatula. Place an inverted plate over the skillet and, grasping skillet and plate firmly together, turn them upside down. The pancake should slip out of the skillet, browned side up.

Spread the meat filling over the first pancake, smoothing it evenly with a spatula and carefully slide the second cake directly on top of it. Cut into pie-shaped wedges and serve at once.

Duszona Wołowina w Potrawce Grzybowej (Poland)
BRAISED BEEF STUFFED WITH MUSHROOMS

To serve 6

BEEF
4 pounds eye of round, about 4
   inches in diameter, tied crosswise
   at 2-inch intervals

2 teaspoons salt
Freshly ground black pepper
2 tablespoons oil
1 cup water

Pat the beef dry with paper towels and sprinkle it on all sides with the 2 teaspoons of salt and a few grindings of pepper. Heat the oil in a heavy 10- to 12-inch skillet and, when it is very hot but not smoking, add the meat. Brown the beef in the hot oil, turning it frequently and regulating the heat so it colors richly and evenly on all sides without burning. Transfer the meat to a heavy casserole large enough to hold it comfortably.

Pour 1 cup of water into the skillet and bring to a boil over high heat, stirring and scraping in the brown particles that cling to the bottom and sides of the pan. Pour the contents of the skillet over the beef, cover the casserole, and simmer over low heat for about 2 hours, or until the interior still shows some resistance when pierced with a sharp knife.

STUFFING
2 ounces imported dried
   mushrooms, preferably Polish
   dried mushrooms, covered with 2
   cups boiling water and soaked for
   at least 4 hours
2 tablespoons unsalted butter
½ cup finely chopped onions

½ teaspoon finely chopped garlic
½ cup dry white bread crumbs
   made from day-old white bread
   with crusts removed
1 egg
1 teaspoon salt
Freshly ground black pepper
2 tablespoons finely chopped parsley

While the meat is simmering, prepare the stuffing. Combine the mushrooms and their soaking liquid in a 1-quart enameled or stainless-steel saucepan. Bring to a boil over high heat, then reduce the heat to low and simmer uncovered for 30 minutes. Pour the contents of the pan into a fine sieve set over a bowl, and set the drained liquid aside. Chop the mushrooms fine.

Heat the butter in a small pan and, when the foam begins to subside, add the chopped onions and garlic. Cook over moderate heat for 2 to 3 minutes, stirring frequently, until the onions are soft and translucent but not brown. Stir in the chopped mushrooms and cook another 2 to 3 minutes. Remove from the heat and cool to room temperature. Then stir in the bread crumbs, egg, 1 teaspoon of salt, a few grindings of black pepper and the parsley. Moisten with 1 tablespoon of the reserved mushroom liquid and taste for seasoning.

When the meat has braised for its allotted time, remove it from the casserole and with a very sharp knife slice it crosswise into 12 thin slices.

Do not cut through the bottom of the meat, but only to within 1 inch of the bottom. Divide the stuffing into six equal portions and spread a portion on every other slice of meat, spreading it as evenly as possible with a small spatula or knife. Slide 2 crisscrossing lengths of string under the bottom of the beef and bring the ends over the top. Knot the cords securely to hold the slices of beef in place. Return the beef to the casserole and pour in the remaining reserved mushroom liquid. Bring to a boil over high heat, reduce the heat to low, cover, and simmer for about 45 minutes, or until the meat is tender. Transfer the beef to a heated platter and drape foil over it to keep it warm while you prepare the sauce.

| 1 tablespoon flour | 1 cup sour cream |
| 2 egg yolks | |

With a large spoon skim off and discard as much fat as possible from the surface of the stock remaining in the casserole. Bring the stock to a simmer over moderate heat. In a small bowl, beat the tablespoon of flour and 2 egg yolks into the sour cream. Beat about ½ cup of the hot stock into the sour-cream mixture, then pour it slowly back into the simmering stock. Stirring constantly, simmer for 2 or 3 minutes, until the sauce thickens lightly. Do not let it come to a boil or it may curdle.

Remove the strings from the beef and cut through every other slice so that each serving portion consists of 2 slices of meat with stuffing between them. Arrange the slices slightly overlapping on a large heated platter and serve at once. Present the sauce separately in a bowl or sauceboat.

Sarmale *(Romania)*
STUFFED CABBAGE LEAVES WITH SAUERKRAUT

To make about 12 cabbage rolls

1 pound fresh sauerkraut	quarter-pound stick), cut into
A 2½- to 3-pound white cabbage,	small bits
raw or fermented *(see note)*	1 cup tomato purée, mixed with
¼ cup long-grain unconverted	1½ cups water
white rice	¼ teaspoon ground hot red pepper
1½ pounds lean ground pork	(cayenne)
3 cups finely chopped onions	1 cup finely chopped green pepper
1 teaspoon crumbled dried thyme	6 lean bacon slices
1½ teaspoons salt	4 tomatoes, cut lengthwise into
8 tablespoons unsalted butter (1	quarters

Drain the sauerkraut, wash it under cold running water, and let it soak in cold water for 10 to 20 minutes, depending upon its acidity. A handful at a time, squeeze the sauerkraut until it is dry. Set aside in a bowl.

Continued on next page

Remove the bruised and tough outer leaves of the cabbage and wash the head under cold running water. Drop it into a large pot of boiling water and cook briskly for about 10 minutes. Remove the cabbage with tongs, but let the water continue to boil. Carefully peel off as many of the outer leaves as you can without tearing them. Then return the cabbage to the boiling water and cook for a few minutes longer. Again peel off the softened outer leaves. Repeat the process until you have detached 12 perfect leaves. Pat them dry with paper towels and set them aside.

Bring 1 quart of water to a boil over high heat and stir in the rice. Boil briskly, uncovered, for 10 minutes, or until partially cooked. Drain the rice in a sieve or colander, run cold water over it and set aside.

Grind the pork together with ½ cup of the onions through the finest blade of a meat grinder into a deep bowl. Add the rice, thyme and salt, knead vigorously with both hands, then beat with a wooden spoon until the mixture is smooth and fluffy.

Lay the cabbage leaves side by side and, with a small knife, trim the base of each leaf of its tough rib end. Place about ½ cup of the pork filling in the center of each leaf (smaller leaves will take less), and roll up each leaf tightly, tucking in the ends to make a neat oblong package.

Preheat the oven to 350°. Melt the butter over moderate heat in a heavy 3- to 4-quart casserole. When the foam begins to subside, add the remaining 2½ cups of onions and, stirring frequently, cook for about 5 minutes, or until they are soft and translucent but not brown. Add the tomato-purée-and-water mixture and ground red pepper and bring to a boil. Then with a fork stir the contents of the pan into the sauerkraut.

Spread about one third of the mixture on the bottom of the casserole. Arrange 6 of the cabbage rolls side by side on top, then sprinkle them with ⅓ cup of the green pepper. Cover the rolls with half of the remaining sauerkraut mixture, arrange the rest of the cabbage rolls on top and again sprinkle them with another ⅓ cup of the green pepper. Add the rest of the sauerkraut mixture and pour in any liquid remaining in the bowl. Sprinkle with the final ⅓ cup of green pepper and arrange the bacon strips on top. Bring to a boil on top of the stove, cover the casserole tightly, and bake in the middle of the oven for 1 hour. Then arrange the tomato quarters in one layer across the top of the bacon, re-cover, and bake ½ hour longer.

Serve at once, directly from the casserole. Pork *sarmale* is traditionally accompanied by *mamaliga (page 89)*.

NOTE: *Sarmale* is characterized in Romania by the acidulated flavor of fermented cabbage leaves. To ferment a cabbage, place it in an 8- to 10-quart casserole and cover with 6 quarts of cold water. Add 1½ cups of salt and bring to a boil. Lower the heat and simmer, partially covered, for 10 minutes. Place a heatproof plate on top of the cabbage to keep it submerged and set it aside for 3 days. Separate the large leaves, drain, and use in place of the fresh cabbage leaves described above.

Carbonnades à la Flamande *(Belgium)*

FLEMISH BEEF-AND-BEER STEW

To serve 4

3 pounds lean boneless beef chuck, sliced ½ inch thick, then cut into strips 2 inches long and 1 inch wide
1 teaspoon salt
Freshly ground black pepper
4 to 6 tablespoons lard
½ pound lean sliced or slab bacon, cut into ¼-inch pieces
4 cups thinly sliced onions (about 1 pound)

½ teaspoon finely chopped garlic
2 tablespoons flour
2 cups (16 ounces) beer, preferably dark beer
1 cup beef stock, fresh or canned
A bouquet of 4 fresh parsley sprigs and 1 medium-sized bay leaf, tied together with string
½ teaspoon crumbled dried thyme
1 teaspoon sugar
2 tablespoons red wine vinegar

Preheat the oven to 350°. Pat the strips of beef completely dry with paper towels and drop them into a bowl. Sprinkle with the salt and a few grindings of pepper and toss the meat about with a wooden spoon until it is evenly seasoned. In a heavy 4- to 5-quart enameled or stainless-steel casserole, melt 4 tablespoons of the lard over high heat until it is very hot but not smoking. Brown the beef in the hot lard, a handful at a time, turning the strips frequently with a slotted spoon and regulating the heat so that they color richly and evenly without burning. As they brown, transfer the pieces of beef to a plate and brown the remaining meat similarly, adding more lard to the pan if necessary.

Drop the bacon bits into the fat remaining in the casserole and, stirring frequently, cook over moderate heat until the bits are brown and crisp and have rendered all their fat. With a slotted spoon, transfer the bacon to paper towels to drain. Pour all but about ¼ cup of fat from the casserole. Add the onions to the casserole. Stirring frequently, cook over moderate heat for about 15 minutes, or until the onions are soft and delicately browned. Add the garlic and stir in the flour with a wooden spoon.

When the flour is completely absorbed, pour in the beer and ½ cup of the beef stock. Bring to a boil over high heat, stirring constantly with a whisk until the sauce thickens. Add the bouquet of parsley and bay leaf, the thyme and sugar, and return the beef and any liquid that has accumulated around it to the casserole. Stir in the bacon. The liquid should completely cover the meat; if necessary add up to ½ cup more of the stock. Cover tightly and place the casserole in the middle of the oven. Bake for 1½ hours, or until the beef is tender. Just before serving, stir in the vinegar and taste for seasoning. Serve at once, directly from the casserole or from a large heated bowl. *Carbonnades à la flamande* is traditionally accompanied by hot boiled potatoes.

Tajin Chakchouka *(Tunisia)*

BAKED LAMB AND CHEESE WITH PEPPERS

To serve 6 to 8

1 pound lean boneless lamb
　shoulder, trimmed of excess fat
　and cut into 1-inch cubes
⅛ teaspoon ground cinnamon
3 teaspoons salt
¼ teaspoon freshly ground black
　pepper
6 tablespoons olive oil
3 cups water
1½ cups finely chopped onions
3 medium-sized firm ripe tomatoes,
　peeled, seeded and coarsely
　chopped *(see bigos, page 80)*
2 medium-sized green bell peppers,
seeded, deribbed and coarsely
　chopped
¼ teaspoon crushed hot red pepper
　flakes
¼ teaspoon *hrisa (page 103)*
¼ teaspoon ground hot red pepper
　(cayenne)
A pinch of dried ground coriander
¼ cup freshly grated imported
　Parmesan cheese
¼ cup soft fresh crumbs made
　from homemade-type white
　bread, pulverized in a blender or
　finely shredded with a fork
6 eggs, lightly beaten
2 tablespoons unsalted butter, melted

Pat the cubes of lamb completely dry with paper towels, then drop them into a bowl and toss them about with the cinnamon, 1 teaspoon of the salt and the black pepper. In a heavy 12-inch skillet, warm 3 tablespoons of the oil over high heat until a light haze forms above it. Brown the lamb in the hot oil, turning the cubes about frequently with a wooden spoon and regulating the heat so they color quickly and evenly without burning. Pour in just enough water to cover the lamb (about 2 cups) and bring to a boil over high heat, stirring constantly and scraping in the brown particles that cling to the pan. Reduce the heat to low and simmer partially covered for 45 minutes. With a slotted spoon transfer the lamb to a 3-quart baking-serving dish. Skim off and discard as much fat as you can from the surface of the sauce and set the skillet aside.

Meanwhile prepare the *chakchouka:* In a heavy 10- to 12-inch skillet, warm the remaining 3 tablespoons of oil over moderate heat. Add the onions and, stirring frequently, cook for about 5 minutes, until they are soft and translucent but not brown. Stir in the tomatoes, green peppers, red pepperflakes, *hrisa,* cayenne, coriander and the remaining 1 cup of water and 2 teaspoons of the salt. Bring to a boil over high heat, reduce the heat to low and, stirring from time to time, simmer for about 15 minutes, or until most of the liquid in the pan has evaporated.

Preheat the oven to 350°. Add the *chakchouka* to the lamb and stir in the cheese and bread crumbs. When the mixture is well blended, stir in the beaten eggs. Taste for seasoning, then bake uncovered in the middle of the oven for about 45 minutes, or until the top is golden brown.

Dribble the melted butter evenly over the top and serve at once, directly from the baking dish. Heat the reserved lamb sauce briefly in the skillet and serve separately in a heated bowl or sauceboat.

Ragoût de Mouton aux Chicons *(Belgium)*

LAMB STEW WITH ENDIVES

To serve 6 to 8

3 pounds lean boneless lamb shoulder, trimmed of excess fat and cut into 1½-inch cubes
2 teaspoons salt
Freshly ground black pepper
4 tablespoons butter
3 tablespoons vegetable oil
1½ cups finely chopped onions
1½ teaspoons finely chopped garlic
3 cups beef stock, fresh or canned

1 cup water
1 small bay leaf
4 whole cloves
2 tablespoons finely chopped fresh parsley
½ teaspoon crumbled dried thyme
2 pounds small new potatoes (12 to 16), each about 2 inches in diameter, peeled and cut in half
6 small Belgian endives
1 tablespoon cornstarch dissolved in 2 tablespoons cold water

Pat the pieces of lamb completely dry with paper towels, place them in a bowl, and sprinkle with the salt and a few grindings of pepper. Toss the meat about gently with a wooden spoon to distribute the seasonings evenly. In a heavy 5- to 6 quart casserole, melt the butter with the oil over high heat. When the foam begins to subside, add 5 or 6 pieces of lamb and turn them frequently with tongs or a slotted spoon, regulating the heat so that the pieces color richly and evenly without burning. As they brown, transfer them to a plate and brown another 5 or 6 pieces.

When all the lamb is browned, pour off and discard all but about 2 tablespoons of the fat from the pot. Add the onions and garlic and, stirring frequently and scraping in the brown particles that cling to the bottom and sides of the casserole, cook over moderate heat for about 5 minutes, or until the onions are soft.

Return the lamb and any liquid that may have accumulated around it to the casserole. Add the beef stock, water, bay leaf, cloves, parsley and thyme and, stirring constantly, bring to a boil over high heat. Reduce the heat to low, cover partially, and simmer for 30 minutes. Add the potatoes and simmer partially covered for 30 minutes longer.

Meanwhile, with a small, sharp knife trim the bases of the endives and wash them under cold running water. (In Belgium, part of the bitter center core at the base is sometimes cut out when the endive is trimmed. You may remove about ¼ inch of the core with a small knife or apple corer, but be careful not to cut so deeply that the leaves spearate.)

Add the endives to the stew and continue to simmer for 15 to 20 minutes more, or until the lamb and vegetables are tender but not falling apart. Stirring constantly, pour in the cornstarch mixture in a thin stream and simmer only long enough for the sauce to thicken lightly. Taste for seasoning and serve the ragout at once, directly from the casserole or arranged attractively on a heated deep platter.

Kouski bil Lahm *(Tunisia)*
COUSCOUS WITH BEEF AND VEGETABLES

To serve 6

COUSCOUS
2 pounds *couscous (see Glossary)*
2½ teaspoons salt dissolved in
    2½ cups cold water

1 tablespoon olive oil
4 tablespoons unsalted butter, cut
    into bits

Spread the *couscous* evenly in a large shallow pan. Sprinkle it with 2 cups of the salted water, then dribble the tablespoon of oil over the top. Rub the moistened grains gently between your palms, dropping the *couscous* back into the pan until the water and oil have been completely absorbed. Cover with foil or plastic wrap and set aside at room temperature for 15 minutes; the pellets will swell slightly.

BEEF AND VEGETABLES
1 cup vegetable oil
2 pounds boneless chuck, cut into
    2-inch cubes and patted dry with
    paper towels
3 cups finely chopped onions
4 teaspoons *hrisa (page 103)*
⅛ teaspoon ground allspice
½ teaspoon salt
Freshly ground black pepper
4 medium-sized carrots, peeled and
    cut crosswise into 2-inch pieces
4 medium-sized turnips, peeled and
    cut into 2-inch pieces
½ cabbage, cored and cut into
    2-inch pieces

½ pound (about 1 cup) dried
    chick-peas *(garbanzos),* soaked
    for 12 hours, drained, rinsed,
    simmered in water to cover for 1
    hour and drained again, or
    substitute 2 cups drained canned
    chick-peas
3 medium-sized firm ripe tomatoes,
    quartered
3 cups cold water
6 medium-sized boiling potatoes,
    peeled
4 small unpeeled zucchini, cut into
    2-inch pieces
1 pound pumpkin, peeled and cut
    into 2-inch pieces

    Meanwhile, in the lower part of a 4-quart *couscoussier* or in a deep 6-quart kettle or casserole, heat 1 cup of oil until a light haze forms above it. Add the cubes of meat and the onions, and sprinkle the meat with the *hrisa,* allspice, salt and a few grindings of black pepper. Fry uncovered over high heat for 6 to 8 minutes, turning the meat over frequently with tongs until it is golden brown on all sides. Add the carrots, turnips, cabbage, chick-peas and tomatoes, pour in 3 cups of cold water (or just enough to cover the meat and vegetables), and stir until the mixture comes to a boil. Reduce the heat to low.

    Set the top part of the *couscoussier* in place. Or set a colander lined with cheesecloth into the kettle or casserole; it should not touch the food in the pot. Twist damp paper towels or kitchen towels into long narrow strips and wrap them around the rim of the *couscoussier* or kettle to seal the joint between the upper and lower parts.

Slowly add about 2 cups of the *couscous* to the upper pot or colander, rubbing the pellets between your palms as you drop them in, and letting them mound naturally. When steam begins to rise through the pellets, add another cup or so of *couscous* in the same manner. Repeat, letting steam appear after each addition. When all the *couscous* has been rubbed into the pot or colander, continue to steam uncovered and undisturbed for 20 minutes. Then remove the top part, return the *couscous* to the shallow pan again, spread it out with a wooden spoon, and set aside to dry.

As the vegetables and meat become tender, transfer them with a slotted spoon to a platter and drape foil over them to keep them warm. Add the potatoes, zucchini and pumpkin to the pot and, if necessary, pour in enough boiling water to cover the vegetables completely. Stirring occasionally, bring to a boil over high heat. Then reduce the heat to low, set the top pot or colander in place again, and let the vegetables cook while you complete the preparation of the *couscous*.

Sprinkle the remaining ½ cup of salted water and the butter bits over the *couscous* and rub the grains gently between your palms as before until the water and butter are completely absorbed.

Again seal the joint at the rim of the pot with the towel strips. Slowly add 2 cups of the *couscous* to the top pot or colander as you did before, rubbing the pellets between your palms as you drop them in, letting them mound naturally, and waiting for steam to appear before adding more. Steam uncovered and undisturbed for about 15 minutes, or until the zucchini is tender but not falling apart. Transfer it with a slotted spoon to the reserved meat and vegetables, then replace the top. Continue to steam the *couscous* undisturbed for another 10 or 15 minutes, or until it is soft but still somewhat resistant to the bite.

To serve, mound the *couscous* on a large heated platter. Return the meat and vegetables to the pot and cook over high heat for 2 to 3 minutes, until they are heated through. Moisten the *couscous* with about 1 cup of the sauce in the pot, and arrange the pieces of meat and vegetables around it. Pour the rest of the sauce into a bowl and stir in the remaining 3 teaspoons of *hrisa*. Serve at once, accompanied if you like by one or more of the traditional Tunisian relishes: potato salad, turnip-and-lime-juice relish, or cucumber relish *(Recipe Index)*.

Bigos (Poland)
HUNTER'S STEW

To serve 4 to 6

4 large imported European dried
  mushrooms, preferably dried
  Polish mushrooms
½ to 1 cup boiling water
1 pound fresh sauerkraut
7 tablespoons butter
1 cup finely chopped onions
1 medium-sized tart cooking apple,
  peeled, cored and coarsely
  chopped
½ pound white cabbage, trimmed,
  cored, washed and finely
  shredded
2 medium-sized firm ripe tomatoes
2 tablespoons vegetable oil
1 pound lean beef chuck, trimmed
  of excess fat and cut into 1-inch
  cubes
½ pound lean boneless venison,
trimmed of excess fat and cut into
  1-inch cubes, or substitute ½
  pound lean boneless lamb,
  trimmed of excess fat and cut into
  1-inch cubes
½ pound lean boneless pork,
  trimmed of excess fat and cut into
  1-inch cubes
½ cup chicken stock, fresh or
  canned
½ cup dry Madeira
½ pound fresh kiełbasa (page
  68), cut into rounds 1 inch
  thick, or substitute fresh or
  smoked commercial kiełbasa, cut
  into 1-inch rounds
4 whole allspice
1½ teaspoons salt
Freshly ground black pepper

Place the dried mushrooms in a small bowl, pour in enough boiling water to cover, and soak for at least 2 hours, or until the mushrooms are soft and flexible. Drain the mushrooms, reserving the soaking liquid, and cut them crosswise into paper-thin slices. Set aside.

Drain the sauerkraut, wash it thoroughly under cold running water and then let it soak in a bowl of cold water for 10 to 20 minutes, depending on its acidity. A handful at a time, squeeze the sauerkraut until it is completely dry. Then pull the strands apart with your fingers.

Drop the tomatoes into boiling water for 15 seconds, then peel off the skin. Cut out the stems and cut the tomatoes in half crosswise. Squeeze the halves to remove the juice and seeds, then coarsely chop the pulp.

In a heavy 4- to 5-quart casserole, melt 4 tablespoons of the butter over moderate heat. When the foam subsides, add the onions and apple. Stirring frequently, cook for about 5 minutes, or until the onions are soft and translucent but not brown. Remove from the heat and stir in the mushrooms, their soaking liquid, the sauerkraut, cabbage and tomatoes.

Preheat the oven to 350°. In a heavy 10- to 12-inch skillet, melt the remaining 3 tablespoons of butter in the vegetable oil over high heat. Brown the beef, venison (or lamb) and pork in the hot fat in separate batches, turning the cubes of meat frequently with tongs or a slotted spoon. As they brown, transfer them to the casserole.

Pour the chicken stock and Madeira into the fat remaining in the skillet and bring to a boil over high heat, stirring constantly and scraping in the brown particles that cling to the pan. With a rubber spatula, scrape the contents of the skillet into the casserole. Add the *kiełbasa,* allspice, salt and a liberal grinding of pepper to the vegetable-and-meat mixture. Cover the casserole tightly and bake in the middle of the oven for 1½ hours. Uncover and continue to bake for 30 minutes longer, or until the meats and vegetables are tender. Taste for seasoning and serve at once, directly from the casserole or from a large heated bowl.

Hutspot met Klapstuk *(Netherlands)*
HOTPOT WITH BOILED MEAT

To serve 4 to 6

1 quart water
2 teaspoons salt
2 pounds fresh brisket of beef, in
   1 piece
2 pounds medium-sized carrots,
   peeled and cut into ½-inch dice

3 pounds boiling potatoes (8 to 9),
   peeled and cut into eighths
3 cups coarsely chopped onions
Freshly ground black pepper
¼ cup spicy brown mustard
   (optional)
Sour pickles (optional)

In a heavy 2½- to 3-quart casserole, bring 1 quart of water to a boil. Add the salt and meat, and bring back to a boil, skimming the surface of the water of any scum or fat that rises to the top. Partially cover the pot, lower the heat, and simmer 2½ to 3 hours, or until the meat shows only the slightest resistance when pierced with the tip of a sharp knife. Check the water frequently; it may be necessary to add up to 2 more cups of boiling water to keep the meat immersed in liquid while it cooks.

Drop in the diced carrots and continue to simmer for another 30 minutes, then add the potatoes and onions. Simmer uncovered until the vegetables are very soft and the cooking liquid has nearly evaporated. Remove the meat from the casserole and set it aside, lightly covered with aluminum foil to keep it warm. Mash the vegetables to a purée in the casserole with a wooden spoon and taste for seasoning. Then transfer the purée to a heated platter and shape it into a mound in the center. With a sharp carving knife, cut the meat against the grain into thin slices and arrange them around the vegetables. Serve at once, accompanied if you like by sharp mustard and pickles.

Sucsu *(Morocco)*

STEAMED COUSCOUS WITH LAMB, VEGETABLES AND RAISINS

To serve 6

COUSCOUS

2 pounds *couscous (see Glossary)*
2½ teaspoons salt dissolved in
 2½ cups cold water

1 tablespoon olive oil
4 tablespoons unsalted butter, cut
 into bits
¼ teaspoon ground cinnamon

Spread the *couscous* evenly in a large shallow pan. Sprinkle it with 2 cups of the salt water, then dribble the 1 tablespoon of olive oil over the top. Rub the moistened grains gently between your palms, lifting and dropping the *couscous* back into the pan, until the water and oil have been completely absorbed. Cover the pan with foil or plastic wrap and set the *couscous* aside at room temperature for 15 to 20 minutes; the pellets will swell slightly.

MEAT AND VEGETABLES

4 tablespoons peanut or vegetable
 oil
2 pounds lean boneless lamb
 shoulder, trimmed of excess fat
 and cut into 1-inch pieces
1 large onion, cut into 1-inch
 chunks
2 large firm ripe tomatoes,
 quartered
1½ teaspoons salt
1 tablespoon freshly ground black
 pepper
1 stick cinnamon, broken in half
¼ cup finely chopped parsley
¼ cup finely chopped fresh
 coriander *(cilantro)*
¼ teaspoon crumbled saffron
 threads or ground saffron
3 cups cold water

½ pound (1 cup) dried chick-peas
 (garbanzos), soaked 12 hours,
 drained, rinsed and simmered in
 water to cover for 1 hour, then
 drained again, or substitute 2
 cups drained canned chick-peas
2 medium-sized carrots, cut in half
 lengthwise, then cut crosswise
 into 2-inch lengths
2 small white turnips, peeled and
 cut into strips ¼ inch wide and
 1 to 2 inches long
½ pound sweet potatoes, peeled
 and thinly sliced
1 pound pumpkin, peeled and cut
 into 1-inch chunks
½ cup seedless raisins
1 pound zucchini, peeled and cut
 crosswise into 1-inch chunks

Meanwhile, in the lower part of a 4-quart *couscoussier* or in a deep 6-quart kettle or casserole, combine the 4 tablespoons of oil, the lamb, onion, tomatoes, salt, pepper, cinnamon sticks, parsley, coriander and saffron. Fry uncovered over high heat for about 5 minutes, turning the lamb chunks over with tongs until they are golden brown all over. Add 3 cups of water (or just enough to cover the meat) and the chick-peas, and stir until the mixture comes to a boil. Reduce the heat to moderate.

Set the top part of the *couscoussier* in place. Or set a colander lined with cheesecloth into the kettle or casserole; it should not touch the food in the pot. Twist damp paper towels or kitchen towels into long narrow strips and wrap them around the rim of the *couscoussier* or kettle to seal the joint between the upper and lower parts.

Slowly add about 2 cups of the *couscous* to the upper pot or colander, rubbing the pellets between your palms as you drop them in and letting them mound naturally. When steam begins to rise through the pellets, add another cup or so of *couscous* in the same manner. Repeat, letting steam appear after each addition. When all the *couscous* has been rubbed into the pot, continue to steam uncovered and undisturbed for 20 minutes. Remove the top part of the *couscoussier,* return the *couscous* to the shallow pan again, spread it out with a wooden spoon, and set aside.

Add the carrots, turnips, sweet potatoes, pumpkin and raisins to the stew and pour in just enough boiling water to cover the vegetables completely. Stirring constantly, bring back to a boil over high heat. Reduce the heat to moderate, set the top pot or colander in place again, and let the vegetables cook while you complete the preparation of the *couscous*.

Sprinkle the remaining ½ cup of salt water, the butter bits and the powdered cinnamon over the *couscous* and rub the grains gently between your palms as before until the water and butter are completely absorbed.

Again seal the joint at the rim of the pot with the towel strips. Slowly add 2 cups of the *couscous* to the top part of the pot or to the colander as you did before, rubbing the pellets between your palms as you drop them in, letting them mound naturally, and waiting for steam to appear before adding the rest, 1 cup at a time. Steam uncovered and undisturbed for about 15 minutes. Remove the top pot and, if the lamb, sweet potatoes and pumpkin are tender, transfer them from the bottom pot with a slotted spoon to a platter and cover with foil to keep them warm. Add the zucchini to the bottom pot. Replace the top and continue to steam the *couscous* undisturbed for another 10 to 15 minutes, or until it is soft but still somewhat resistant to the bite.

To serve, mound the *couscous* on a large heated platter. Return the meat and vegetables to the stew and cook over high heat for 2 or 3 minutes, until heated through. Taste for seasoning, then moisten the *couscous* with about 1 cup of the lamb sauce. With the back of a large spoon, make a round depression in the center of the *couscous* and drop in the vegetables and raisins. Arrange the meat in a ring around the *couscous*. Pour the remaining sauce into a bowl and present it separately. Serve at once.

Berneplatte *(Switzerland)*

SIMMERED MIXED MEATS WITH STRING BEANS AND POTATOES

To serve 8 to 10

2 pounds fresh lean brisket of beef, trimmed of excess fat

2½ to 3 pounds uncooked smoked pork loin, cut into 1-inch-thick chops (about 10 chops)

1 pound slab bacon, preferably double smoked, with rind removed, cut into slices ¼ inch thick and about 4 inches long

8 to 10 knackwurst

8 to 10 uncooked pork sausages

8 to 10 small frankfurters or Vienna sausages

2 quarts lightly salted boiling water

2 pounds trimmed fresh green string beans

4 tablespoons butter

4 tablespoons flour

½ teaspoon finely chopped garlic

⅛ teaspoon ground nutmeg, preferably freshly grated

½ teaspoon salt

10 to 12 boiling potatoes (about 4 pounds), peeled and boiled in salted water until tender

Place the brisket in a 5- to 6-quart heavy pot and pour in enough cold water to cover it by at least 2 inches. Bring to a boil over high heat, skimming off the foam and scum as they rise to the surface. Reduce the heat to low and simmer partially covered for 1½ hours. Add the smoked pork loin and bacon, partially cover the pot, and simmer for 15 minutes longer. Add the knackwurst and pork sausages and cook for 10 minutes. Then drop in the small frankfurters or Vienna sausages and let them simmer slowly for about 5 minutes. (All the meats should be completely covered with water throughout the cooking period; replenish the pot with boiling water whenever necessary.)

Meanwhile prepare the green beans. Bring 2 quarts of lightly salted water to a boil in a 3- to 4-quart saucepan. Drop in the beans and cook briskly, uncovered, for 10 to 15 minutes, until they are tender but still slightly crisp. Drain the beans in a sieve set over a bowl and set aside the cooking liquid. Run cold water over the beans, and set aside.

In a heavy 8- to 10-inch skillet, melt the butter over moderate heat. When the foam subsides, stir in the flour and continue to stir until the mixture is smooth. Pour in 2 cups of the string bean liquid and, stirring constantly, cook over high heat until the sauce comes to a boil and thickens heavily. Reduce the heat to low, add the garlic, nutmeg and salt, and simmer for about 5 minutes, stirring occasionally. Add the beans to the sauce and simmer only long enough to heat them through. To serve, carve the brisket into slices ¼ inch thick. Slice the knackwurst or the pork sausage into serving pieces if you like or serve them whole. Spread the string beans and their sauce on a large heated serving platter. Arrange the meats attractively over the beans, surround with the potatoes, and serve at once.

Vegetables and Grains

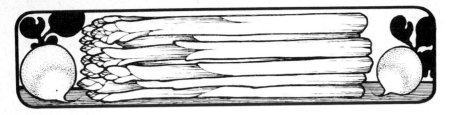

Dulma (Tunisia)
ZUCCHINI STUFFED WITH LAMB AND RICE

To serve 4 to 6

12 small zucchini or other summer
   squash
½ pound lean ground lamb
1 cup finely chopped onions
6 tablespoons cooked rice, made
   from 2 tablespoons long-grain
   unconverted rice, or 6
   tablespoons leftover boiled rice
2 eggs
¼ cup finely chopped fresh parsley

1 teaspoon finely cut fresh mint
   leaves, or substitute ½ teaspoon
   crumbled dried mint
¼ teaspoon *hrisa (page 103)*
⅛ teaspoon ground mace
1 teaspoon salt
½ cup olive oil
4 medium-sized firm ripe tomatoes,
   peeled *(see bigos, page 80)* and
   quartered
½ cup water
½ teaspoon freshly ground black pepper

Scrub the zucchini under cold running water and pat them dry with paper towels. With a small, sharp knife, cut about ½ inch off both ends of
each zucchini. Carefully tunnel out the center of each zucchini, leaving a
¼-inch-thick shell all around. The best utensil for this is the Syrian *mu-
nara,* or squash corer, but an apple corer is almost as effective.

In a deep bowl, combine the lamb, ½ cup of the onions, the rice,
eggs, parsley, mint, *hrisa,* mace and salt. Knead the ingredients together
with your hands, then beat vigorously with a wooden spoon until the mixture is smooth. Taste for seasoning. Stuff the zucchini with the lamb mixture, dividing it evenly among them and smoothing the open ends with
a spatula.

Warm the oil in a heavy 12-inch skillet over moderate heat. When a
light haze forms above it, add the remaining ½ cup of onions and, stirring frequently, cook for about 5 minutes, until they are soft and
translucent but not brown. Stir in the tomatoes, water and pepper, and
bring to a boil over high heat. Arrange the zucchini in one layer on top of
the tomatoes, and spoon the liquid over them. Reduce the heat to low,
cover tightly, and simmer for about 20 minutes, or until the zucchini are
tender enough to be easily pierced with a fork.

To serve, arrange the zucchini attractively on a heated platter and pour
the tomato sauce over them.

Asperges de Malines *(Belgium)*
ASPARAGUS WITH EGG SAUCE

To serve 4

2 hard-cooked eggs, coarsely
chopped
1 tablespoon finely chopped fresh
parsley

½ teaspoon plus 3 tablespoons salt
⅛ teaspoon white pepper
12 tablespoons unsalted butter
(1½ quarter-pound sticks),
melted and cooled
2½ to 3 pounds fresh asparagus

In a small mixing bowl, stir the chopped eggs, parsley, ½ teaspoon of salt and the pepper together with a fork until they are well combined. Then, stirring constantly, pour in the butter in a thin stream. Cover the bowl tightly with foil or plastic wrap and set the sauce aside.

Lay the asparagus spears side by side on a board and trim their bases with a sharp knife. Ideally, all spears should be the same length. With a small, sharp knife—not a vegetable parer—peel each spear, starting at the base. At the base end the peeling may be as thick as ⅟₁₆ inch, but it should gradually become paper thin as the knife cuts and slides toward the tip. Be careful not to cut off the tips. When all the spears are peeled, wash them under cold running water.

In an 7- to 8-quart enameled or stainless-steel casserole, bring 6 quarts of water and 3 tablespoons of salt to a vigorous boil over high heat. Drop in the asparagus and boil uncovered and undisturbed for 8 to 10 minutes, or until the ends are tender but still slightly resistant when pierced with a small, sharp knife. Do not overcook.

With tongs, transfer the asparagus spears to a large heated platter and serve at once, accompanied by the egg sauce in a separate bowl.

Ardei cu Untdelemn *(Romania)*
PEPPERS IN OIL

To serve 4 to 6

6 medium-sized bell peppers, green
or red
½ cup olive oil
½ cup white wine vinegar
½ cup cold water
2 teaspoons imported paprika

1 tablespoon salt
Freshly ground black pepper
12 ripe black olives, preferably
Mediterranean type
Brynza cheese, or substitute *feta*
cheese, cut into 1-inch cubes
8 to 12 scallions, trimmed and
washed

Roast the peppers in the following fashion: Impale them, one at a time, on the tines of a long-handled fork and turn over a gas flame until the skin blisters and darkens. Or place the peppers on a baking sheet and broil them 3 inches from the heat for about 15 minutes, turning them so that they color on all sides. As the peppers are roasted, wrap them in a damp towel and let them rest for 5 minutes. Rub them with the towel until the burned skins slip off, but leave the stems intact.

In a deep bowl combine the olive oil, vinegar, water, paprika, salt and a few grindings of pepper. Beat vigorously with a whisk or a fork until the ingredients are combined, then taste for seasoning. Add the peppers and turn them about with a spoon until they are coated on all sides.

Marinate at room temperature for 3 or 4 hours, turning the peppers over occasionally. Then cover the bowl tightly with foil or plastic wrap and refrigerate for at least 24 hours before serving. Peppers in oil are traditionally served on a platter, moistened with some of their marinade and garnished with black olives, cheese and scallions.

Serve as a salad course or as an accompaniment to *mititei (page 70)*.

Riebeles *(Switzerland)*
FRIED CORNMEAL CAKES

To make about 12 two-inch-square cakes

2 tablespoons butter, softened, plus	1 tablespoon vegetable oil
2 to 6 tablespoons butter	½ pound yellow cornmeal (about
2 cups milk	1⅓ cups)
2 cups water	2 teaspoons salt

With a pastry brush, spread the 2 tablespoons of softened butter evenly over the bottom and sides of an 8- or 9-by-6-inch shallow baking dish. Set aside.

In a heavy 3- to 4-quart saucepan, bring the milk, water and oil to a boil over high heat. Stirring constantly with a wooden spoon, pour in the cornmeal in a slow, thin stream so that the water continues to boil as the cornmeal is absorbed. Then reduce the heat to low and, stirring frequently, simmer for 15 to 20 minutes, or until the cornmeal is so thick that the spoon will stand unsupported in the middle of the pan.

While the cornmeal is still hot, spoon it into the buttered dish, spreading it out to a ½-inch thickness and smoothing the top with a spatula. Cover with wax paper and refrigerate for at least 6 hours or overnight, until the cornmeal is firm to the touch.

With a pastry wheel or a sharp knife divide the chilled cornmeal into 2-inch squares and carefully lift them out of the baking dish with a small metal spatula. In a heavy 10- to 12-inch skillet, melt 2 tablespoons of butter over moderate heat. When the foam begins to subside, add 4 or 5 of the *riebeles* to the skillet and brown them for 2 or 3 minutes on each side, turning them over gently with a spatula. Fry the remaining *riebeles* similarly, adding the remaining butter if necessary. Serve at once, as an accompaniment to sausages, bacon or fried ham. *Riebeles* are a traditional Swiss breakfast dish.

Ghiveciu National *(Romania)*
FRESH VEGETABLE STEW WITH VEAL AND GRAPES

*Although the Romanians traditionally use a great variety of colorful vege-
tables in their national stew, you may, if you wish, eliminate some, in-
creasing the quantity of others. For example, you may omit the acorn
squash or cauliflower and double the amount of potatoes or eggplant.*

To serve 6 to 8

¾ pound fresh pork fat, cut into
   small dice, or 8 tablespoons
   melted butter combined with 4
   tablespoons vegetable oil
3 pounds boneless breast of veal, cut
   into 1-inch chunks
2 tablespoons salt
Freshly ground black pepper
½ cup flour
3 medium-sized onions, peeled and
   cut into ¼-inch-thick slices
2 teaspoons coarsely chopped garlic
4 cups freshly made beef stock, or
   substitute 2 cups condensed
   canned beef stock combined with
   2 cups cold water
2 tablespoons tomato paste
1 small eggplant (about ¾ to 1
   pound), peeled
6 medium-sized boiling potatoes
   (about 2 pounds), peeled

½ small white cabbage (about ½
   pound), trimmed and cored
1 pound acorn squash, peeled and
   seeded
3 medium-sized carrots (about ½
   pound), peeled
1 large green bell pepper, stemmed,
   deribbed and seeded
1 medium-sized celery root
   (celeriac), about ½ pound, peeled
1 small cauliflower (about ¾ to 1
   pound), trimmed and washed
¼ pound green string beans,
   trimmed, and cut in half lengthwise
1 cup dry red wine
2 teaspoons finely chopped parsley
½ teaspoon crumbled dried marjoram
½ teaspoon crumbled dried thyme
4 medium-sized firm ripe tomatoes,
   peeled, cut into quarters and seeded
   (*see bigos, page 80*)
¼ pound seedless green grapes, washed
¼ cup fresh green peas, shelled

Preheat the oven to 350°. In a heavy 12-inch skillet, fry the pork fat (if
you are using it) over moderate heat, stirring frequently, until it is crisp,
delicately browned, and has rendered all its fat. Remove the crisp bits
with a slotted spoon and discard them. Pour the rendered fat into a measuring cup; there should be about ¾ cup. Pour 4 tablespoons of the fat
back into the skillet and set aside off the heat.

Pat the chunks of veal completely dry. Season them on all sides with 1
teaspoon of the salt and a liberal grinding of pepper. Dip them in the
flour and, when they are evenly coated, shake vigorously to remove the excess flour. Heat the pork fat in the skillet over high heat until a drop of
water flicked into it splutters and evaporates instantly. Or, pour 4 tablespoons of the butter-and-oil mixture into a 12-inch skillet and place
over high heat until the foam begins to subside. Brown the veal chunks
in the hot fat, 7 or 8 at a time, turning them frequently with tongs or a
spatula. Add more fat or butter and oil to the skillet as needed. As the
veal browns, transfer the chunks to a heavy 6- to 8-quart casserole.

Add the onion slices and garlic to the fat remaining in the skillet and, stirring frequently, cook for about 5 minutes, until they are soft and translucent. With a slotted spoon transfer the onions and garlic to the casserole and spread them over the veal. Pour off all the fat from the skillet and in its place add 1 cup of the stock (or the stock-and-water mixture) and the tomato paste. Stirring constantly, bring to a boil over high heat. Pour the mixture into the casserole.

Cut the eggplant, potatoes, cabbage and squash into 1½-inch cubes, and cut the carrots, green pepper and celery root into strips about 2 inches long and ¼ inch wide. Separate the cauliflower into small flowerets.

Put 6 tablespoons of pork fat or butter and oil in the skillet and place it over moderate heat. Adding them to the skillet in separate batches and frying each batch just long enough to color the pieces lightly and evenly, fry the eggplant, potatoes, carrots, string beans, green pepper, celery root, squash, cauliflower and cabbage. As they brown, transfer the vegetables to the casserole with a slotted spoon, arranging each one in a separate layer. Add more fat to the skillet when necessary.

Pour off any fat remaining in the skillet, then add the remaining 3 cups of stock (or stock and water), the wine, parsley, marjoram, thyme and remaining salt. Bring to a boil over high heat, scraping in any browned particles clinging to the bottom and sides of the skillet. Pour the mixture down the sides of the casserole. Bring to a boil over high heat, then cover tightly and bake in the middle of the oven for 45 minutes. Add the tomatoes, grapes and peas, and bake covered for 15 minutes longer. Taste for seasoning, then serve directly from the casserole.

Mamaliga *(Romania)*
CORNMEAL PORRIDGE

To serve 8

	2⅔ cups finely ground yellow or
1 quart water	white cornmeal
1 tablespoon salt	4 tablespoons butter, melted

In a heavy 2- to 3-quart saucepan, bring the water and salt to a boil over high heat. Pour the cornmeal very slowly into the boiling water, making sure that the boiling never stops and stirring constantly with a wooden spoon to keep the mixture smooth. Reduce the heat to low, cover tightly, and simmer for 10 to 12 minutes, or until the *mamaliga* is very thick and all the liquid in the pan has been absorbed.

Serve at once, mounded on a heated platter and moistened with the melted butter. *Mamaliga* may be served with meat and gravy as a substitute for bread or potatoes; or it may be served at room temperature as a separate course surrounded by black olives, hard-cooked eggs, dill and tarragon sprigs and accompanied by sour cream and *brynza* cheese.

Vegetarianski Palachinki *(Bulgaria)*
HERB PANCAKES

To make about 16 small pancakes

3 eggs
1 cup finely chopped fresh parsley
½ cup finely chopped scallions, including 2 inches of the green tops

½ cup finely cut fresh dill leaves
1 teaspoon salt
Freshly ground black pepper
3 tablespoons butter
2 tablespoons vegetable oil

With a whisk or fork, beat the eggs together in a bowl until they are well blended. Stir in the parsley, scallions, dill, salt and a few grindings of black pepper. Taste for seasoning. In a heavy 10- to 12-inch skillet, melt the butter with the oil over moderate heat. When the foam begins to subside drop about 2 tablespoons of the egg-and-herb mixture into the pan and flatten it into a pancake about 2 inches in diameter. Make about 4 or 5 more pancakes in similar fashion leaving about an inch between them in the pan. Fry for 2 or 3 minutes on each side, or until the pancakes are golden brown and crisp around the edges. Place the finished pancakes side by side on a heated platter and set aside while you fry the rest, adding more butter and oil to the pan when necessary.

When all the pancakes are done, serve at once as a vegetable accompaniment to meats, poultry or fish.

Chicorée et Volaille Bruxelloise *(Belgium)*
BRAISED ENDIVES STUFFED WITH CHICKEN

To serve 6 as a first course

4 tablespoons unsalted butter, softened, plus 4 tablespoons unsalted butter
6 large firm endives, with tightly closed unblemished leaves
Salt
White pepper
¼ cup strained fresh lemon juice
A 6- to 8-ounce chicken breast, skinned and boned

¼ cup flour
1 cup chicken stock, fresh or canned
1 cup heavy cream
⅛ teaspoon ground nutmeg, preferably freshly grated
1 egg yolk
½ cup freshly grated imported Gruyère cheese
6 slices boiled ham, each ⅛ inch thick and about 6 inches wide and 8 inches long

Preheat the oven to 325°. With a pastry brush, spread 2 tablespoons of the softened butter evenly over the bottom and sides of a baking-serving dish large enough to hold the endives in one layer.

With a small, sharp knife trim off the bases of the endives (making sure not to cut so deep that the leaves separate) and wash the endives under cold running water. Pat them completely dry with paper towels, then arrange them side by side in the buttered dish and with a pastry brush spread them with the remaining 2 tablespoons of softened butter. Sprinkle the endives with ½ teaspoon salt and ¼ teaspoon of white pepper, and pour the lemon juice over them.

Cover the endives with a sheet of wax paper cut to fit flush with the inside rim of the dish. Then bake in the middle of the oven for about 1½ hours, or until the bases of the endives are tender and show no resistance when pierced deeply with the point of a skewer. With tongs or a slotted spatula carefully transfer the endives to a plate. Pour off any liquid remaining in the dish and set the dish aside.

Raise the oven temperature to 375°. In a small flameproof baking pan, melt 1 tablespoon of the butter over moderate heat. When the foam begins to subside, add the chicken breast and turn it about with a spoon until it glistens on all sides. Remove the pan from the heat, sprinkle the chicken with ¼ teaspoon salt and ⅛ teaspoon white pepper, and cover it with wax paper cut to fit inside the pan. Poach the chicken in the middle of the oven for 8 to 10 minutes, or until the flesh feels firm to the touch. Transfer the chicken to a plate and, with a sharp knife, cut it into ¼-inch dice. Place the diced chicken in a small bowl and set aside.

In a heavy 1½- to 2-quart saucepan, melt the remaining 3 tablespoons of butter over moderate heat, stir in the flour, and mix thoroughly. Pour in the chicken stock and, stirring constantly with a wire whisk, cook over high heat until the sauce thickens heavily and comes to a boil. Reduce the heat to low and simmer for about 5 minutes to remove any taste of raw flour, then stir in the cream, nutmeg, ¼ teaspoon of salt and a pinch of white pepper. Taste for seasoning and add more salt or pepper if necessary. Pour about ¼ cup of the sauce over the reserved chicken dice and mix well. Then beat the egg yolk into the remaining sauce and when it is completely absorbed stir in the cheese.

Increase the oven heat to 400°. With a sharp knife, slit each endive in half lengthwise, cutting to within about 1 inch of the base. One at a time, spread the endives open butterfly fashion and flatten one half gently with the side of a cleaver or large knife. Divide the chicken mixture into 6 equal portions. Spread one portion of the chicken mixture on the flattened sides of each endive, then fold the other half of the endive over the filling and wrap each stuffed endive securely in a slice of ham.

Arrange the wrapped endives side by side (seamed side down) in the baking-serving dish and spoon the reserved sauce evenly over the top. Bake in the middle of the oven for about 10 minutes, or until the sauce begins to bubble. Then place the baking dish under a preheated broiler (about 3 inches from the heat) for a minute or so to brown the sauce further. Serve at once, directly from the baking dish.

Ardei Umplut cu Orez *(Romania)*
STUFFED GREEN PEPPERS IN TOMATO SAUCE

To serve 6

6 large green peppers (about ¼
   pound each) stemmed, seeded
   and deribbed
1 tablespoon plus 1½ teaspoons salt
1 cup long-grain unconverted white
   rice
5 tablespoons butter
1 cup plus 2 tablespoons finely
   chopped onions
4 tablespoons finely chopped fresh
   parsley

2 tablespoons finely cut fresh fennel
   leaves, or substitute ½ teaspoon
   powdered fennel
Freshly ground black pepper
1 egg, lightly beaten
1 tablespoon flour
½ cup chicken stock, fresh or canned
4 medium-sized firm ripe tomatoes,
   peeled, seeded and coarsely
   chopped *(see bigos, page 80)*
6 tablespoons sour cream

Preheat the oven to 350°. Drop the peppers into a pot with enough boiling water to cover them completely and boil briskly for 2 or 3 minutes. Cover the pot, remove it from the heat, and set aside for 5 minutes. Then, with tongs or a slotted spoon, remove the peppers from the water and invert them on paper towels to drain.

Bring 2 quarts of water with 1 tablespoon of salt to a boil in a saucepan and, stirring constantly, pour in the rice. Boil briskly, uncovered, for 10 minutes. Then drain the rice in a sieve or colander, run cold water over it, and set it aside.

In a heavy 8- to 10-inch skillet, melt 3 tablespoons of the butter over moderate heat. When the foam begins to subside, add 1 cup of the onions and, stirring frequently, cook for about 5 minutes, until they are soft and translucent but not brown. Watch carefully for any sign of burning and regulate the heat accordingly. Remove the skillet from the heat and stir in the rice, 2 tablespoons of the parsley, the fennel, 1 teaspoon of the salt and a few grindings of pepper. When all the ingredients are thoroughly mixed, cool to room temperature, then stir in the egg. Set aside.

Melt the remaining 2 tablespoons of butter over moderate heat in a heavy 2- to 3-quart casserole large enough to hold the peppers upright side by side. Add the remaining 2 tablespoons of onions and fry for 2 or 3 minutes, until they are soft but not brown. Then add the flour and mix together thoroughly. Pour in the stock and, stirring constantly with a whisk or spoon, cook over high heat until the sauce comes to a boil. Reduce the heat to low, simmer for about 3 minutes, and stir in the tomatoes and the remaining ½ teaspoon of salt. Remove from the heat.

Spoon the rice mixture into the peppers, dividing it evenly among them and tamping it down with the back of a spoon. Top each pepper with 1 tablespoon of sour cream and sprinkle the cream with the remaining 2 tablespoons of parsley. Arrange the peppers upright in the casserole, cover tightly, and bake in the middle of the oven for 30 minutes, or until the peppers are soft and show no resistance when their skins are pierced with the point of a small, sharp knife. Serve at once, directly from the casserole.

Meh-lakh *(Tunisia)*
PICKLED VEGETABLES

To make about 2 quarts

4 cups red or wine vinegar
¼ cup salt
3 medium-sized celery stalks, trimmed and with leaves removed, cut into strips about 1½ inches long and ¼ inch wide (1 cup)
2 medium-sized carrots, scraped and cut into strips 1½ inches long and ¼ inch wide (1 cup)

½ pound medium-sized white turnips, peeled and cut into strips 1½ inches long and ¼ inch wide (1 cup)
1 small zucchini (about ½ pound), peeled and cut into strips 1½ inches long and ¼ inch wide (1 cup)
½ pound cauliflower, separated into flowerets

Combine the vinegar and salt in a deep bowl and stir with a wooden spoon until the salt dissolves. Add the celery, carrots, turnips, zucchini and cauliflower, and turn them about to coat them well. With a slotted spoon, transfer the vegetables to two 1-quart canning jars, dividing the mixture evenly between them. Pour the brine into the jars, cover tightly with lids, and let the vegetables pickle at room temperature for 5 days before serving. They may then be kept for 2 or 3 weeks, either in the refrigerator or at room temperature. *Meh-lakh* is usually served as an accompaniment to apéritifs, especially *boukha* (fig brandy).

Stampot van Boerenkool met Worst *(Netherlands)*
KALE WITH POTATOES AND SAUSAGE

To serve 6

2 pounds fresh kale
6 small baking potatoes (about 2 pounds), peeled and cut into 1-inch cubes
2 cups milk

4 tablespoons lard
1 teaspoon salt
Freshly ground black pepper
A 1-pound precooked fresh or smoked sausage, such as *kiełbasa* (*page 68*)

Wash the kale thoroughly under cold running water. With a small, sharp knife, cut away the ends, the tough stems and any bruised or yellow leaves. Drop the kale into enough lightly salted boiling water to cover it completely, then reduce the heat to moderate and cook uncovered for 30 minutes. Add the potatoes and cook for 30 minutes longer, or until the

Continued on next page

kale is tender. The potatoes should still be intact. Remove them with a slotted spoon and set them aside. Transfer the kale to a colander to drain, and press the leaves firmly with the back of a spoon to remove any excess liquid; then chop the kale coarsely.

In a heavy 2- to 3-quart saucepan, heat the milk and lard over moderate heat, stirring frequently, until the lard is melted and small bubbles appear around the edge of the pan. Stir in the kale, potatoes and salt, and reduce the heat to low. Cover tightly and simmer for about 20 minutes. Taste for seasoning and add as much freshly ground pepper as you like.

Meanwhile, with the point of a small knife, prick the sausage in 5 or 6 places to prevent the skin from bursting and so that it will release its fat when it cooks. Lay the sausage flat in a large skillet and add enough cold water to cover it completely. Bring to a boil over moderate heat, reduce the heat to low, and simmer for about 10 minutes. Transfer the sausage to paper towels to drain, then split the skin with a sharp knife and peel it off. Cut the sausage crosswise into ¼-inch-thick rounds.

To serve, mound the kale and potatoes in the middle of a large deep platter and arrange the sausage attractively around the rim.

Pommes à la Liégeoise (Belgium)
BAKED POTATOES WITH JUNIPER-BUTTER SAUCE

To serve 4

4 medium-sized baking potatoes
  (about ½ pound each)
  thoroughly scrubbed
½ pound unsalted butter, cut into
  ½-inch bits
4 teaspoons finely chopped shallots
2 teaspoons finely chopped garlic
16 whole juniper berries, bruised
with the flat of a cleaver or large
  knife
2 tablespoons strained fresh lemon
  juice
1 teaspoon salt
¼ teaspoon white pepper
2 tablespoons finely cut fresh chives
2 tablespoons finely chopped fresh
  parsley

Preheat the oven to 425°. Place the potatoes on a wire rack set in a shallow roasting pan and bake in the middle of the oven for 40 minutes to 1 hour, or until they show only the slightest resistance when squeezed gently between your thumb and forefinger.

Meanwhile, in a small, heavy skillet or saucepan, melt the butter over moderate heat, stirring it from time to time to prevent it from browning. Watch carefully for any sign of burning, and regulate the heat accordingly. Add the shallots, garlic and juniper berries, and stir for 2 or 3 minutes, until the shallots are soft but not brown. Remove the pan from the heat and stir in the lemon juice, salt and pepper. Taste for seasoning.

To serve, cut a 2-inch cross in the top of each potato and press the sides gently to split the potato apart. Spoon the juniper-butter sauce (reheated if necessary) into the openings of the potatoes and sprinkle the tops with chives and parsley.

Rösti *(Switzerland)*
FRIED SHREDDED POTATO CAKE

To serve 4 to 6

9 medium-sized baking potatoes (about 3 pounds)

½ teaspoon salt
¼ cup vegetable oil
2 tablespoons butter

Drop the potatoes into enough boiling water to cover them completely and cook briskly for about 10 minutes, or until the point of a knife can be inserted about 1 inch into a potato before meeting any resistance. Drain the potatoes. When cool enough to handle, peel them with a small, sharp knife, cover with plastic wrap, and refrigerate for at least an hour. Just before frying the potatoes grate them into long strips on the tear-shaped side of a four-sided stand-up grater. Toss lightly with the salt.

In a heavy 10-inch slope-sided skillet (preferably one with a nonstick cooking surface), heat the oil and butter over moderate heat until a drop of water flicked over them splutters and evaporates instantly. Drop in the potatoes and, with a spatula, spread them evenly in the pan. Fry uncovered for 8 to 10 minutes, using a spatula to gently lift up a side of the potatoes to check their color as they brown. When the underside of the potato cake is as brown as you can get it without letting it burn, place a plate upside down over the skillet. Grasping the skillet and plate firmly together, invert them quickly. Then carefully slide the potato cake, browned side up, back into the skillet. (If you are not using a pan with a nonstick surface, add more butter and oil before returning the potatoes to the pan.) Fry for 6 to 8 minutes, or until the bottom side of the potatoes is as evenly browned as the top and the edges are crisp.

Slide the potato cake onto a heated platter and serve at once.

NOTE: *Rösti* potatoes are often made with onions or bacon. Sauté ½ cup of finely chopped onions in 3 tablespoons of butter until they are soft and transparent. Drop half the shredded potatoes into the skillet, pat them flat and smooth and spread the onions evenly over them before adding the remaining potatoes, patting them down as before. Or fry ½ cup of finely diced bacon until the bits are crisp, drain on paper towels and spread the bacon over half of the potatoes as described for the onions.

Patates Frites (Belgium)
BELGIAN-STYLE FRENCH FRIED POTATOES

Admittedly, rendering kidney fat for French fried potatoes takes more time than frying the potatoes in vegetable oil. But the extra effort is rewarding because the beef fat gives the potatoes a characteristic Belgian flavor impossible to achieve in any other way. Moreover, the fat is quite inexpensive, and when strained and refrigerated can be reused several times to deep-fry not only potatoes but other foods as well.

To serve 6

5 pounds beef kidney suet, cut into ¼-inch dice	9 medium-sized boiling potatoes (about 3 pounds)
1 cup cold water	Salt

Combine the suet and water in a heavy 4- to 5-quart casserole and bring to a boil over high heat, stirring frequently. Reduce the heat to the lowest possible point, cover tightly, and simmer for about 2 hours, or until the solid bits of suet are crisp and a delicate golden color and have rendered all their fat.

Let the fat cool for 5 to 10 minutes, then strain it into a deep bowl or pan through a fine sieve lined with a double layer of dampened cheesecloth. With a wooden spoon, gently press the solid bits to remove all their fat before discarding them. There should be at least 2 quarts of fat.

Peel the potatoes and drop them into a bowl of cold water to prevent their discoloring. With a large, sharp knife, cut the potatoes lengthwise into slices about ⅜ inch thick, then cut the slices into strips about ⅜ inch wide and 2½ to 3 inches long. As you cut each strip, return it to the cold water.

Pour the fat into a deep fryer or large heavy saucepan to a depth of at least 4 to 6 inches and heat it to 325° on a deep-frying thermometer.

A handful at a time, pat the potato strips completely dry with paper towels and plunge them into the hot fat. Turning the strips about with a slotted spoon, fry the potatoes for 8 minutes. Then transfer them to paper towels to drain. Deep-fry and drain the remaining potatoes similarly. The partially fried potatoes can wait unrefrigerated for several hours, or you may complete their frying at once.

Just before serving, heat the fat once more, but this time let it reach a temperature of 360°. A handful at a time, deep-fry the potatoes for about 2 minutes, turning them about with a slotted spoon, until they are crisp and brown. Drain the *patates frites* on paper towels and sprinkle them lightly with salt.

NOTE: Although it is less traditional, the potatoes may be successfully deep-fried in vegetable oil. Heat the oil to 325° for the preliminary frying, and allow each batch to cook for 6 to 7 minutes. Heat the oil to 375° for the final frying, and allow about 2 minutes for the potatoes to crisp and turn brown.

Racuchy *(Poland)*
GRATED POTATO PANCAKES

To make about 14 pancakes

4 medium-sized baking potatoes
    (about 1½ pounds), peeled
1 medium-sized onion, peeled
1 egg, separated
1 tablespoon potato flour, or
    substitute 2 tablespoons

all-purpose flour
1 teaspoon salt
¼ teaspoon ground white pepper
1 tablespoon finely chopped fresh
    parsley
Vegetable oil
1 cup applesauce (optional)

Set a large sieve over a mixing bowl and grate the potatoes on the finest side of a stand-up grater directly into the sieve. Then grate the onion over the potatoes and, with the back of a large spoon, press as much liquid as possible from the mixture. Set aside the drained liquid in the mixing bowl and transfer the grated potatoes and onions to a large bowl. Add the egg yolk, flour, salt and pepper and, with a wooden spoon, beat vigorously until the ingredients are thoroughly combined.

Pour off the drained liquid in the mixing bowl without disturbing the layer of potato starch that will have settled on the bottom. Add the starch to the potato mixture and stir thoroughly.

In a small bowl, beat the egg white with a wire whisk or a rotary or electric beater until it forms unwavering peaks on the beater when lifted from the bowl. With a rubber spatula, scoop the egg white over the potato mixture and fold them together gently but thoroughly. Fold in the chopped parsley.

Preheat the oven to its lowest setting and line a large shallow baking dish with a double thickness of paper towels. Place the baking dish in the center of the oven.

Pour enough vegetable oil into a heavy 10- to 12-inch skillet to come ¼ inch up the sides of the pan. Warm the oil over high heat until a drop of water flicked into it splutters and evaporates instantly. For each pancake, drop about 1 tablespoon of the batter into the skillet and flatten it gently into a 2½- to 3-inch cake. Fry 4 or 5 pancakes at a time, for about 2 minutes on each side, or until they are golden brown and crisp around the edges. As they brown, transfer the *racuchy* to the lined dish and keep them warm in the oven while you fry the rest.

To serve, arrange the pancakes on a heated platter and, if you like, sprinkle them with a little salt. Present the applesauce separately in a small bowl. *Racuchy* may be served as an accompaniment to roast loin of pork *(Recipe Index)*, brisket of beef or poultry.

Salads and Relishes

How to Prepare and Seal Canning Jars

To ensure consistent results in canning fruits and vegetables, use standard canning jars with matching lids and airtight seals. Wash the jars, lids and rings in hot, soapy water and rinse them with scalding water. Place them in a large, deep pot and pour in enough hot water to submerge them completely. Bring to a boil over high heat, then turn off the heat and let the pan stand while you finish cooking the food to be canned. The jars must be hot when the food is placed in them.

When the food is ready for canning, remove the jars from the pot with tongs and stand them upright on a level surface. Leave the lids and rings in the pot until you are ready to use them. Fill the jars one at a time, and seal them quickly and tightly with the rings and lids.

Marynowane Śliwki (Poland)
PICKLED PLUMS

To·make about 1 quart

1 pound small firm purple plums	2½ cups sugar
4 cups distilled white vinegar	3 whole cloves
4 cups cold water	½ teaspoon ground cinnamon

Wash the plums under cold running water, pat them completely dry with paper towels and place them in a large glass or ceramic bowl.

In a 1½- to 2-quart enameled or stainless-steel saucepan, bring 2 cups of the vinegar and 2 cups of the water to a boil over high heat. Pour the boiling liquid over the plums and let them soak at room temperature for about 1 hour. Then pour the liquid back into the same saucepan, bring it to a boil, and pour it over the plums again; set them aside to soak for 1 hour longer. Drain off the liquid and discard it.

Pour the remaining 2 cups of vinegar and 2 cups of water into the saucepan. Add the sugar, cloves and cinnamon, and bring to a boil over high heat, stirring until the sugar dissolves. Pour the liquid over the plums and set them aside to cool to room temperature.

With a slotted spoon, pack the plums into a 1-quart canning jar, following the directions for canning and preserving above. Return the soaking liquid to the saucepan and bring it back to a boil. Pour the boiling liquid over the plums, a little at a time, filling the jar to within ¼ inch of the top. Seal at once. Let the plums pickle at room temperature for at least 2 weeks before serving them as an accompaniment to such roast meats as loin of pork with applesauce glaze *(Recipe Index)*.

Torshi *(Tunisia)*
TURNIP-AND-LIME-JUICE RELISH

To serve 4 to 6

1 tablespoon strained fresh lime
    juice
1 teaspoon salt

4 medium-sized white turnips,
    peeled and cut crosswise into ⅛-
    inch-thick rounds
1 teaspoon *hrisa (page 103)*

In a serving bowl, stir the lime juice and salt together until the salt is dissolved. Drop in the turnips and turn them about with a spoon. When they are evenly coated with the lime mixture, cover tightly with foil or plastic wrap and marinate at room temperature for at least 3 hours. Just before serving, stir in the *hrisa. Torshi* is traditionally served in Tunisia as an accompaniment to *kouski bil lahm (Recipe Index)*.

Msir *(Morocco)*
SALTED LEMONS

To make 4 preserved lemons

4 lemons

2 teaspoons salt

With a small, sharp knife, slice each of the lemons lengthwise into quarters, cutting to within about ½ inch of the bottom so that the segments are not completely separated. Sprinkle the cut surfaces evenly with the salt and reassemble the lemons, pressing them gently into their original shape. Place the lemons in a canning jar large enough to hold them compactly, cover tightly with the lid, and marinate at room temperature for at least 2 weeks. Discard the juice that has accumulated in the jar and completely separate the lemons into quarters. The salted lemons are used in *tajine* such as *tajine msir zitum* and *el lahm el m'qali (Recipe Index)*.

Surówska z Kiszonej Kapusty *(Poland)*
SAUERKRAUT SALAD WITH CARROTS AND APPLES

To serve 4

¼ cup vegetable oil
1 teaspoon caraway seeds
1 teaspoon sugar
½ teaspoon salt

1 pound fresh sauerkraut
1 medium-sized tart cooking apple,
   peeled, cored and cut into
   ½-inch dice (1 cup)
2 carrots, scraped and coarsely
   grated (1 cup)

In a large serving bowl, combine the vegetable oil, caraway seeds, sugar and salt. Beat briskly with a fork or spoon until the sugar and salt are completely dissolved.

Drain the sauerkraut, wash it thoroughly under cold running water, and let it soak in a bowl of cold water for 10 to 20 minutes, depending upon its acidity. A handful at a time, squeeze the sauerkraut until it is dry, then chop it as fine as possible.

Add the sauerkraut, apple and carrots to the oil mixture and toss them together lightly but thoroughly with a fork. Taste for seasoning and refrigerate until ready to serve.

Meshana Salata *(Bulgaria)*
MIXED PEPPER-AND-WALNUT SALAD

To serve 4

4 medium-sized green bell peppers
   (about 1 pound)
1 tablespoon plus ½ cup olive oil
1 cup finely chopped onions
2 ounces walnuts, pulverized in a

blender or ground with a nut
grinder or mortar and pestle
(½ cup)
½ teaspoon finely chopped garlic
1 teaspoon salt
Freshly ground black pepper
6 tablespoons red wine vinegar

Preheat the oven to 300°. Following the directions for peppers in oil *(page 86)*, roast and peel the peppers. Remove the stems and cut the peppers lengthwise into quarters. Discard the seeds and cut away the white membrane. Then slice the peppers lengthwise into ½-inch-wide strips.

Pour 1 tablespoon of the oil into a shallow baking dish large enough to hold the pepper strips in one layer and tip the dish from side to side to spread the oil evenly. Arrange the pepper strips in the dish, sprinkle the onions evenly over them, and bake in the middle of the oven for 30 minutes, or until the peppers are soft. With a rubber spatula transfer the peppers and onions to a bowl and set them aside to cool to room temperature.

Meanwhile, with a mortar and pestle or in a small bowl using the back of a spoon, pound or mash the walnuts, garlic, salt and a few grindings of black pepper to a smooth paste. Beat in the remaining ½ cup of olive oil, 1 tablespoon at a time, and when the mixture is as smooth as possible stir in the vinegar a tablespoon at a time. Taste for seasoning.

Pour the walnut sauce over the peppers and toss together gently but thoroughly. Serve at room temperature, or refrigerate for at least 4 hours and serve chilled.

Mizeria *(Poland)*
CUCUMBERS IN SOUR-CREAM-AND-DILL SAUCE

To serve 4	2 tablespoons distilled white vinegar
2 medium-sized cucumbers	¼ teaspoon sugar
2 teaspoons salt	1 tablespoon finely cut fresh dill
⅓ cup sour cream	leaves

With a small, sharp knife, peel the cucumbers and slice them in half lengthwise. Scoop out the seeds by running the tip of a teaspoon down the center of each half. Cut the cucumbers crosswise into paper-thin slices and spread the slices in one layer in a large shallow glass dish. Sprinkle with salt and set aside at room temperature for 20 minutes.

In a small serving bowl, stir the sour cream, vinegar and sugar together until they are well combined. A handful at a time, squeeze the cucumber slices gently to remove the excess liquid, pat them completely dry with paper towels and drop them into the sour-cream mixture. Then turn the slices about with a spoon until they are evenly coated with the sauce. Taste for seasoning. Cover tightly with foil or plastic wrap and refrigerate for about 2 hours. Just before serving, sprinkle with the dill.

Salatit Batata *(Tunisia)*
POTATO SALAD WITH CARAWAY

To serve 4 to 6	2 tablespoons strained fresh lemon juice
	1 teaspoon *hrisa (page 103),* dissolved
4 medium-sized boiling potatoes,	in 1 tablespoon water
peeled and cut into ¼-inch dice	1 teaspoon ground caraway seeds
½ cup vegetable oil	1½ teaspoons salt

Drop the potatoes into enough lightly salted boiling water to cover them completely and cook briskly, uncovered, until they are tender but still intact. Drain off the water and, sliding the pan back and forth constantly, cook over low heat for a minute or so, until the potatoes are dry.

Meanwhile, in a heavy 10- to 12-inch skillet, warm the oil over moderate heat until a light haze forms above it. Add the lemon juice, the *hrisa*-water mixture, caraway and salt and, stirring constantly, cook until most of the liquid in the pan has evaporated. Remove from the heat, add the potatoes, and turn them about gently with a spoon until they are evenly coated with the seasoned oil. Taste for seasoning. Then transfer to a serving bowl and cool to room temperature before serving. *Salatit batata* is often served in Tunisia with *kouski bil lahm (Recipe Index).*

Slata Mechouia *(Tunisia)*
ROASTED-TOMATO-AND-PEPPER SALAD

To serve 4 to 6

4 large firm ripe tomatoes
3 large green bell peppers
3 tablespoons strained lemon juice
1½ teaspoons salt

Freshly ground black pepper
½ cup finely chopped onions
3 tablespoons olive oil
12 black olives, preferably the
Mediterranean variety

Preheat the oven to 400°. Place the tomatoes and peppers side by side on a large baking sheet and, turning them frequently so they color on all sides, roast in the middle of the oven for 20 minutes. Remove the tomatoes but continue roasting the peppers for about 20 minutes longer, turning them from time to time. Meanwhile, with a small, sharp knife, peel the tomatoes and slice them in half crosswise. Squeeze the halves gently to remove the seeds and juice and chop the tomatoes fine.

When the peppers are evenly colored, wrap them in a damp towel and let them rest for 5 minutes. Then rub the peppers with the towel until the skins slip off. Cut out the stems and white membranes, discard the seeds, and chop the peppers fine.

In a serving bowl, stir the lemon juice, salt and a few grindings of pepper together. Add the tomatoes, peppers and onions, and toss gently but thoroughly. Taste for seasoning. Then dribble the olive oil over the surface of the salad and scatter the black olives on top.

Slata mechouia is traditionally served as a first course, or as an accompaniment to *brik (pages 105, 108 and 109)* or to fried or broiled fish.

Liutenitsa *(Bulgaria)*
SWEET- AND HOT-PEPPER RELISH

To make about 2 cups

1 pound Italian-type sweet green
  frying peppers
1 pound hot red chilies *(see note
  above, opposite)*

7 tablespoons red wine vinegar
4 tablespoons olive oil
1 cup finely chopped onions
1½ teaspoons finely chopped
  garlic
4 teaspoons salt

Following the directions for peppers in oil *(page 86)*, roast and peel the peppers and chilies. Cut the peppers and chilies into halves and remove and discard the stems, white membranes and seeds.

Purée the peppers into a bowl by forcing them through a food mill or rubbing them through a medium sieve with the back of a spoon. Add 3 tablespoons of the vinegar, 2 tablespoons of the oil, ½ cup of the onions, 1 teaspoon of the garlic and 2 teaspoons of the salt, and beat vigorously together with a wooden spoon.

Purée the chilies into a separate bowl precisely as you did the peppers. Add the remaining 4 tablespoons of vinegar, 2 tablespoons of oil, ½ cup of onions, ½ teaspoon of garlic and 2 teaspoons of salt, and beat vigorously with a spoon until the mixture is smooth. Mound the chili purée in the center of a large serving plate and ring it with the green pepper purée. Refrigerate until ready to serve. Traditionally, *liutenitsa* is accompanied by black bread and served with drinks or as a first course.

NOTE: The volatile oils in hot chilies can make your skin tingle and your eyes burn. It is best to handle them with rubber gloves; be careful not to touch your face or eyes. After handling hot chilies it is important to wash your hands with warm water and soap.

Hrisa (Tunisia)
RED PEPPER SPICE

To make about ¾ cup

	¼ cup ground cumin
½ cup ground hot red pepper (cayenne)	2 teaspoons salt

Combine the red pepper, cumin and salt in a small bowl and stir until thoroughly blended. Pour the *hrisa* into an 8-ounce jar or bottle equipped with a tight-fitting lid. Cover and store in a cool place until ready to use.

Shlada dyal Fejjel ou Lichine (Morocco)
RADISH-AND-ORANGE SALAD

To serve 4 to 6

6 tablespoons strained lemon juice
2 tablespoons sugar
⅛ teaspoon salt
10 large firm red radishes, trimmed, washed and coarsely grated
4 medium-sized temple or navel oranges, peeled and with all the outside membranes removed

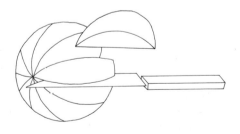

To section an orange, use a small, very sharp knife and cut deeply into the peel near the stem. Cut the peel and all of the white membrane away from the orange, using short sawing motions. Now cut along each side of each membrane division to the core of the orange. As each orange section is freed, carefully lift it out *(above)*. Combine the lemon juice, sugar and salt in a small serving bowl and stir vigorously until the sugar and salt dissolve. Add the radishes and oranges, and toss together gently but thoroughly. Serve at once, or refrigerate until ready to serve. Tightly covered and refrigerated, the salad can keep for 6 to 8 hours.

Pfepfel bar Labid *(Tunisia)*
CUCUMBER-AND-PEPPER RELISH

To serve 4 to 6

2 medium-sized cucumbers
1 tablespoon strained fresh lime
   juice
1 teaspoon salt

2 green bell peppers, sliced
   lengthwise into halves, seeded,
   deribbed and cut into 2-inch
   squares

With a small, sharp knife, peel the cucumbers and slice them lengthwise into halves. Scoop out the seeds by running the tip of a teaspoon down the center of each half. Then cut the cucumbers into 2-inch lengths.

In a serving bowl, stir the lime juice and salt together until the salt dissolves. Drop in the cucumbers and peppers, and turn them about with a spoon. When they are evenly coated with the lime mixture, cover tightly with foil or plastic wrap and marinate at room temperature for at least 8 hours before serving. *Pfepfel bar labid* is traditionally served in Tunisia with *kouski bil lahm (Recipe Index)*.

Kiopoolu *(Bulgaria)*
EGGPLANT AND PEPPER SPREAD

To make about 2 cups

A 1½-pound eggplant
2 medium-sized green peppers,
   roasted, peeled and deribbed *(see
   peppers in oil, page 86)*
1 medium-sized firm ripe tomato,
   peeled, seeded and finely chopped

(see bigos, page 80)
¼ cup olive oil
3 tablespoons red wine vinegar
3 tablespoons finely chopped fresh
   parsley
2 teaspoons finely chopped garlic
1 tablespoon salt
Freshly ground black pepper

Roast the eggplant in the following fashion: Prick it in 3 or 4 places, then impale it on a long-handled fork and turn it over a flame until the skin chars and cracks. Or, pierce the eggplant, place it on a baking sheet, and broil it 4 inches from the heat for about 20 minutes, turning it so that it chars on all sides. Wrap the eggplant in a damp towel for 5 minutes, then peel off and discard the skin. Cut the eggplant in half, chop it fine, and mash the pulp to a smooth purée. Similarly, mash the skinned and deribbed green peppers.

Combine the eggplant and pepper purée in a deep bowl. Stir in the oil and vinegar a tablespoon at a time, then beat vigorously with a wooden spoon until the mixture is smooth. Add the chopped tomato, parsley, garlic, salt and a liberal grinding of pepper, and continue to beat until all the ingredients are well mixed. Taste for seasoning and refrigerate until chilled. Serve mounded on a platter as a first course or spread on dark bread as an accompaniment to drinks.

Breads and Brik

Brik bil Anchouwa *(Tunisia)*
ANCHOVY-AND-CHEESE TURNOVERS

To make 4

FILLING

A 4-ounce can of flat anchovy fillets, drained and soaked at least 4 hours in cold water, or substitute 4 ounces canned tuna, packed in oil

¼ cup finely chopped onions

3 tablespoons finely chopped fresh parsley

2 tablespoons capers, drained and rinsed in a sieve under cold water

¼ teaspoon freshly ground black pepper

1 tablespoon unsalted butter, plus 4 tablespoons unsalted butter, melted (only if using *filo* sheets)

1 tablespoon freshly grated imported Parmesan cheese

Drain the anchovies, pat them completely dry with paper towels and chop them fine. (Or drain the tuna and flake it fine with a fork.) Combine the anchovies (or tuna), onions, parsley, capers and pepper in a bowl and stir until well mixed.

In a heavy 8- to 10-inch skillet, melt 1 tablespoon of butter over moderate heat. When the foam begins to subside, add the fish mixture and, stirring frequently, cook for 2 or 3 minutes. Remove the skillet from the heat and stir in the grated cheese.

BRIK

4 circles *malsouqua (page 106)*, or substitute 4 sheets *filo* pastry, each about 16 inches long and 12 inches wide, thoroughly defrosted if frozen *(see Glossary)*

4 small cold eggs

1 egg, lightly beaten (only if using *filo* sheets)

⅓ cup olive oil

1 lemon, cut lengthwise into quarters

Assemble, cook and serve the *brik* following the directions for *brik bil lahm (page 108)* and using the pastries, eggs, olive oil and lemon specified in the ingredient list above.

Malsouqua (Tunisia)
SEMOLINA PASTRY ROUNDS

"Malsouqua" are round, paper-thin pastries used to make Tunisian "brik" and Moroccan "bastila." Commercial "filo" pastry can be substituted very successfully, but the delicate crispness and flavor of "malsouqua" are preferred. Making them with predictable results can, however, require considerable practice and patience.

To make about 12 rounds

½ cup olive oil	⅛ teaspoon salt
2 cups fine yellow semolina	1⅔ cups cold water

Fill a deep pot about 8 to 9 inches in diameter with enough water to come about ¾ of the way up the sides. Invert a heavy 10-inch skillet with a clean unscratched bottom (or preferably a copper crêpes suzette pan) over the pot, and bring the water to a boil over high heat, thus allowing the surface of the inverted pan to become as hot as possible. Have a large kettle of water simmering on a nearby burner to replenish the water in the pot as it boils away, and place the following within easy reach: the olive oil, a pastry brush, a small mixing bowl filled with cold water, a thin-bladed knife, paper towels, a damp kitchen towel and two spread-out dry kitchen towels.

Now make the batter and fry the pastry in the following fashion: Pour the semolina into a cake pan 10 to 12 inches in diameter (or use a wide baking dish instead). Add the salt and ½ cup of the cold water. Begin stirring the mixture with your hand and continue to stir for about 5 minutes, or until the semolina has absorbed the water. Still stirring, slowly add ¼ cup more of the water; after that has been absorbed, stir in the remaining water in small amounts. When all the water has been used, the

batter will begin to develop small bubbles on its surface as you stir. At this point, change your stirring motion to a clutching and releasing one and manipulate the batter in this manner until it becomes elastic and falls from your fingers in ribbonlike strands *(photograph 1)*. This process should take about 15 minutes from start to finish.

When the batter has reached the desired consistency, dip the pastry brush into the olive oil and very lightly and evenly brush the entire surface of the heated inverted pan. Wipe with a paper towel, leaving only the faintest film of oil on the pan. First dip your hand into the bowl of cold water, then, palm side down, scoop up a handful of the batter, continuously releasing and clutching the dough. With the same movements —as if you were manipulating a Yo-Yo—first smear 2-inch-long streaks around the circumference of the pan. Then continue with similar dabbing movements all over the rest of the pan *(2)*.

As soon as the pan is entirely covered with the lightest, translucent film of batter, quickly wipe your batter-covered hand on the dampened towel and, before the *malsouqua* becomes the slightest bit dry, with your knife cut around the sides of the pan with small slashing motions until you have loosened the edges of the pastry *(3)*. Immediately slide the edge of the knife under the pastry and with both hands carefully and gently peel off the circle *(4)*. If at any point the pastry sticks to the pan, slide the knife under it to detach it. If there are any large holes in the pastry, replace the pastry round on the pan and with your index finger, dab some of the batter over the opening to patch it. Use the edge of the knife to lift the *malsouqua* off the pan again.

Lay the pastry on one of the dry kitchen towels and loosely cover it with the other towel. With a paper towel, clean the surface of the pan, brush it lightly with oil, and wipe as before. Make similar rounds of pastry with the remaining batter, and make a stack of the finished rounds. If one or more of the *malsouqua* are torn beyond repair, set them aside. They can be torn up and used to strengthen *brik (pages 105, 108 and 109)*.

You may use the *malsouqua* at once, or brush their edges lightly with oil, wrap in a towel, and then wrap in aluminum foil. Refrigerated, they will keep for 2 or 3 days.

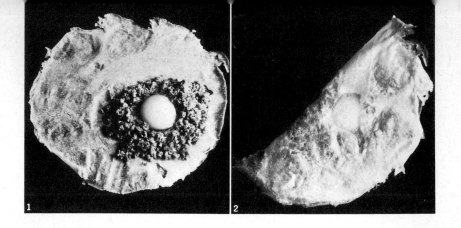

Brik bil Lahm *(Tunisia)*
GROUND LAMB TURNOVERS

To make 4

½ pound lean ground lamb
¼ cup very finely chopped onions
2 tablespoons finely chopped fresh
   parsley
½ teaspoon salt
¼ teaspoon freshly ground black
   pepper
2 tablespoons unsalted butter
4 tablespoons unsalted butter,
   melted (only if using *filo* sheets)

2 teaspoons freshly grated imported
   Parmesan cheese
4 circles of *malsouqua (page 106)*,
   or substitute 4 sheets *filo* pastry
   (see Glossary), each about 16
   inches long and 12 inches wide,
   thoroughly defrosted if frozen
4 small eggs
1 egg, lightly beaten (only if using
   filo sheets)
⅓ cup olive oil
1 lemon, cut lengthwise into quarters

Combine the lamb, onions, parsley, salt and pepper in a deep bowl, and knead vigorously with both hands. Then beat with a wooden spoon until the mixture is smooth and fluffy. In a heavy skillet, melt 2 tablespoons of butter over moderate heat. When the foam subsides, add the lamb mixture and, mashing frequently with the back of a fork to break up lumps of meat as they form, cook until no trace of pink remains. Remove the skillet from the heat and stir in the cheese. Taste for seasoning.

To assemble with *malsouqua:* Spoon a quarter of the lamb filling onto the bottom half of 1 pastry round. Make a well in the mound of lamb and crack 1 egg directly into it, making certain that the egg remains intact *(above, 1)*. Fold the exposed half of the *malsouqua* over the egg and lamb *(2)*; do not be concerned if the edges do not seal. Repeat to make three more *brik*. (If the rounds have holes in them you can, before filling, patch them with pieces torn from extra rounds that are imperfect.)

To assemble with *filo* pastry: Spread 1 sheet flat and brush the top with 1 tablespoon of the melted butter. Fold the sheet in quarters to create a rectangle 8 by 6 inches. Brush again with butter and fold in one of

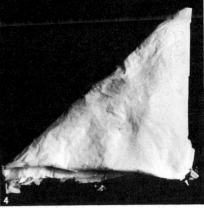

the 8-inch sides by 2 inches to make a perfect 6-inch square. Spoon a quarter of the lamb filling onto the center of one corner of the square, make a well in the mound of lamb, and crack an egg directly into it *(3)*. Brush the edges of the square lightly with the beaten egg and fold the square in half diagonally to create a triangle *(4)*, pressing the edges down firmly to seal them. Repeat the procedure to make three more *brik*.

To fry the *brik,* heat the olive oil in a heavy 8- to 9-inch skillet until it is very hot but not smoking. Slide two of the *brik* at a time into the hot oil and fry them for 2 to 3 minutes on each side, turning them carefully with a wide slotted spatula. When the *brik* are golden brown, transfer them to paper towels to drain while you fry the remaining two. Serve the *brik* while they are still hot, accompanied by the lemon quarters.

Brik di Djaj *(Tunisia)*
CHICKEN TURNOVERS

To make 8

FILLING
2 small boiling potatoes, peeled	A 1-pound chicken breast
1 small onion, peeled and quartered	1 egg
12 sprigs fresh parsley, tied together	¼ teaspoon freshly ground black
1 teaspoon salt	pepper

Combine the potatoes, onion and parsley in a 2-quart saucepan and pour in enough boiling water to cover them by 1 inch. Add the salt and boil briskly for 15 minutes. Then add the chicken breast, reduce the heat to low, and simmer partially covered for about 20 minutes, or until the chicken is white and feels firm to the touch. Pour the contents of the saucepan into a sieve, and drain thoroughly. With a small knife, remove the skin and bones from the chicken and discard them. Chop the chicken meat, po-

Continued on next page   109

tatoes, onion and parsley fine and place them in a bowl. Drop in the egg and pepper, and toss together gently but thoroughly. Taste for seasoning; the mixture may need more salt.

BRIK

8 circles *malsouqua (page 106)*, or substitute 8 sheets *filo* pastry, each about 16 inches long and 12 inches wide, thoroughly defrosted if frozen *(see Glossary)*

4 tablespoons unsalted butter, melted (only if using *filo* sheets)

1 hard-cooked egg, peeled and finely chopped

1 egg, lightly beaten

⅓ cup olive oil

2 lemons, cut lengthwise into quarters

Assemble, cook and serve the *brik,* following the directions for *brik bil lahm (page 108)* and using the pastries, egg, olive oil and lemons specified above. (Note that the chopped hard-cooked egg in this recipe replaces the whole eggs used in *brik bil lahm.)*

Khliab Raiska Ptitsa *(Bulgaria)*
BIRD-OF-PARADISE BREAD

To make 1 round loaf

1 package active dry yeast

½ teaspoon sugar

¼ cup lukewarm water (110° to 115°)

3 to 3½ cups all-purpose flour

2 teaspoons salt

½ cup unflavored yoghurt

4 eggs

2 ounces *brynza* or *feta* cheese *(see Glossary),* rubbed through a sieve or food mill (½ cup)

1 tablespoon salted butter, softened

1 egg lightly beaten with 1 tablespoon milk

¼ pound Kashkaval *(see Glossary),* or substitute sweet Münster cheese, sliced ¼ inch thick and trimmed into 4 triangles about 4 inches long

A ¼-inch-thick slice boiled ham, cut into four 1-inch squares

4 ripe black olives, preferably Mediterranean type

A 1-inch square of sweet red pepper or pimiento, cut into a star

In a small, shallow bowl sprinkle the yeast and sugar over ¼ cup of lukewarm water. Let the mixture stand for 2 or 3 minutes, then stir well. Set the bowl in a warm, draft-free place (such as a turned-off oven) for about 5 minutes, or until the mixture almost doubles in volume.

Combine 3 cups of flour and the salt in a deep mixing bowl, make a well in the center, and pour in the yeast mixture, yoghurt, eggs and *brynza* or *feta* cheese. With a large spoon, gradually stir the flour into the other ingredients, continuing to stir until the mixture is smooth and the flour is completely absorbed. The dough should be just firm enough to be gathered into a ball. If it is too soft, add the remaining ½ cup of flour a tablespoon at a time, beating vigorously after each addition and using only enough of the flour to give the dough its proper consistency; it should not be too firm.

On a lightly floured surface, knead the dough by pushing it down with the heels of your hands, pressing it forward, and folding it back on itself. Continue the kneading for about 10 minutes, or until the dough is smooth and elastic. Sprinkle it from time to time with a little flour to prevent it from sticking to the board.

Shape the dough into a ball and place it in a lightly greased bowl. Drape with a kitchen towel and set aside in a warm, draft-free place for about 1 hour, or until the dough doubles in bulk.

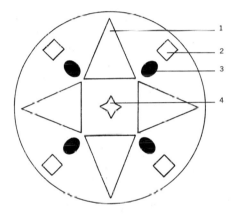

With a pastry brush, spread a large baking sheet with the tablespoon of softened butter. Punch the dough down with a single blow of your fist, shape it into a round loaf about 8 inches in diameter, and set the round on the buttered sheet. Brush the entire surface of the dough evenly with the egg-and-milk mixture, then, following the diagram *above,* arrange the cheese triangles (1), the ham cubes (2), olives (3) and red pepper or pimiento (4) attractively on top. Set the dough aside in a warm place for about 30 minutes to allow it to double in bulk.

Preheat the oven to 400°. Bake the bread in the middle of the oven for 15 minutes, then reduce the heat to 350° and bake for 30 to 40 minutes longer, or until the loaf is golden brown. Transfer the bread to a cake rack to cool. Serve at room temperature.

Birnbrot (Switzerland)

PEAR BREAD

To make 1 loaf

BREAD
1 package active dry yeast
1 teaspoon plus ¼ cup sugar
½ cup lukewarm milk (110° to
   115°)

2 to 2½ cups all-purpose flour
¼ cup vegetable shortening
1 egg
⅛ teaspoon salt
1 teaspoon butter, softened

In a deep mixing bowl, sprinkle the yeast and 1 teaspoon of sugar over the lukewarm milk. Let the mixture stand for 2 or 3 minutes, then stir well. Set the bowl in a warm, draft-free place such as an unlighted oven for about 5 minutes, or until the yeast bubbles up and the mixture almost doubles in bulk.

Stirring constantly, slowly add ½ cup of the flour. Beat in the vegetable shortening and then add the egg, the remaining ¼ cup of sugar and the salt. Beating well after each addition, stir in up to 2 cups more flour, adding it ½ cup at a time and using only as much as necessary to make a dough that can be gathered into a compact ball. If the dough becomes difficult to stir, work in the flour with your fingers.

On a lightly floured surface, knead the dough by folding it end to end, then pressing it down and pushing it forward several times with the heel of your hand. Sprinkle the dough with a little extra flour when necessary to prevent it from sticking. Repeat for about 10 minutes, or until the dough is smooth and elastic.

Shape the dough into a ball and place it in a large bowl coated with 1 teaspoon of butter. Dust the top with a little flour, drape a kitchen towel over the bowl, and set in a warm, draft-free spot for 45 minutes to an hour, until the dough doubles in bulk.

FILLING
1½ cups water
1½ cups coarsely chopped dried
   pears (about ½ pound)
½ cup coarsely chopped, pitted
   dried prunes (about ¼ pound)
½ cup seedless raisins
2 tablespoons strained fresh lemon
   juice
½ cup finely chopped walnuts

6 tablespoons sugar
2 tablespoons imported kirsch
1 teaspoon finely grated fresh lemon
   peel
¼ teaspoon ground cinnamon
¼ teaspoon ground nutmeg
2 to 4 tablespoons dry red wine
1 tablespoon butter, softened
1 egg beaten lightly with 1
   tablespoon milk

Meanwhile prepare the filling in the following fashion: Bring the water to a boil in a small enameled or stainless-steel saucepan. Add the pears, prunes, raisins and lemon juice and, stirring frequently, simmer over low heat for 10 minutes, or until the fruit is tender and can easily be mashed with the back of the spoon.

Drain the fruit thoroughly, then purée it through a food mill or use the back of a spoon to rub it through a sieve set over a bowl. Add the walnuts, sugar, kirsch, lemon peel, cinnamon and nutmeg. When all the ingredients are well mixed, stir in 2 tablespoons of the red wine. The filling should be thick enough to hold its shape almost solidly in a spoon. If it seems too firm, stir in up to 2 tablespoons more wine, a teaspoon or so at a time.

With a pastry brush coat a large baking sheet or jelly-roll pan evenly with the tablespoon of softened butter. Punch the dough down with a single blow of your fist. Transfer it to a lightly floured surface and roll it into a 15-inch square no more than ¼ inch thick.

With a spatula, spread the filling over the dough, covering it smoothly to within 1 inch of the edges. Fold the edges over the filling to make a perfect 13-inch square, then roll the dough jelly-roll fashion into a tight cylinder 12 inches long and about 3 inches in diameter.

Transfer the roll to the buttered baking sheet and lightly prick the outside surface all over with the tines of a fork. Set the roll aside to rise for about 1 hour.

Preheat the oven to 350°. Brush the top, sides and ends of the bread with the egg-and-milk mixture and bake in the middle of the oven for 30 to 35 minutes, or until the bread is golden brown and crisp. Transfer to a wire cake rack to cool. Serve the pear bread warm or at room temperature.

Candies and Desserts

Torta Romaneasca *(Romania)*
LEMON RUM SOUFFLÉ

To serve 6 to 8

14 tablespoons unsalted butter,
softened
1½ cups confectioners' sugar
8 eggs, separated
¼ cup strained fresh lemon juice
1 tablespoon finely grated fresh
lemon peel

¼ cup dark rum, or substitute
cognac
2 tablespoons soft fresh bread
crumbs made from homemade-
type white bread, trimmed of
crusts and pulverized in a blender
or finely shredded with a fork

Preheat the oven to 350°. Fold a 24-inch-long piece of wax paper length-wise in half and again lengthwise in half. With a pastry brush, spread 2 tablespoons of the softened butter evenly on one side of the folded strip, and over the bottom and sides of a 2-quart soufflé dish. Then wrap the paper strip, buttered side in, around the outside of the soufflé dish to make a collar extending about 2 inches above the top edge of the dish. Tie the paper in place with string. Set aside.

In a deep mixing bowl, cream the remaining 12 tablespoons of butter and the sugar together, beating and mashing them against the sides of the bowl with a large spoon until the mixture is light and fluffy. Beat in the egg yolks, one at a time, then stir in the lemon juice, lemon peel and rum. Continue to beat until the ingredients are thoroughly combined.

With a wire whisk or a rotary or electric beater, beat the egg whites until they are stiff enough to stand in unwavering peaks on the beater when it is lifted from the bowl. Fold the egg whites gently into the lemon mixture with a rubber spatula, using an over-under cutting motion rather than a stirring motion. Finally fold in the bread crumbs.

Ladle the soufflé into the buttered and collared dish, spreading it even-ly and smoothing the top with the spatula. Bake in the middle of the oven for 45 minutes, or until the soufflé puffs up above the rim of the col-lar and the top is lightly browned. Carefully remove the wax paper and serve the soufflé at once.

Leniwe Pierogi *(Poland)*
POACHED CHEESE DUMPLINGS

To make about 18 dumplings

¾ pound farmer cheese, crumbled
3 eggs, separated
2 tablespoons sugar
2 tablespoons unsalted butter,
   softened

⅔ cup flour
½ teaspoon salt
8 tablespoons (1 quarter-pound
   stick) unsalted butter, cut in
   ½-inch bits
½ cup dry bread crumbs

With the back of a spoon, rub the farmer cheese thoroughly through a fine sieve into a deep bowl. Beat in the egg yolks one at a time, then the sugar and softened butter. Sift the flour over the cheese mixture and stir vigorously until the flour is completely absorbed.

In a mixing bowl, beat the egg whites with a wire whisk or a rotary or electric beater until they are stiff enough to form unwavering peaks on the beater when it is lifted from the bowl. Scoop the egg whites over the cheese mixture and fold them together gently but thoroughly.

Roll the dough between your palms into 3 equal balls and, on a lightly floured surface, shape each ball into a cylinder about 12 inches long and 1 inch in diameter. Wrap in wax paper and refrigerate for 30 minutes, or until firm. Then flatten the cylinders slightly and cut each of them crosswise into six 2-inch rounds.

In a 3- to 4-quart saucepan, bring 2 quarts of water and the salt to a boil over high heat. Drop 6 of the dumplings into the water, stirring gently so they do not stick to the pan or one another. Immediately reduce the heat to low and poach the dumplings for about 5 minutes, or until they feel firm when prodded gently with a finger. With a slotted spoon, transfer the dumplings to a kitchen towel to drain. Cover them loosely with another towel to keep them warm while you poach the remaining dumplings.

Meanwhile, in an 8-inch skillet, melt the butter bits over moderate heat but do not let the butter brown. Add the bread crumbs and, stirring almost constantly, fry until they are crisp and golden brown. Remove the pan from the heat.

To serve, arrange the dumplings on a large heated platter and pour the browned crumbs and butter over them. *Leniwe pierogi* may be served as a dessert or as a light luncheon dish.

Lichine ma Zhar *(Morocco)*
ORANGE SECTIONS WITH ORANGE-BLOSSOM WATER

To serve 4

4 medium-sized temple or navel
  oranges, peeled, with all of the
  outside membranes removed, and
  divided into sections *(see radish-*

and-orange salad, page 103)
¼ teaspoon orange-blossom water
  (see Glossary)
1 tablespoon confectioners' sugar
⅛ teaspoon ground cinnamon

Arrange the orange sections attractively in rows or concentric circles on a serving plate, overlapping them slightly. Sprinkle them with the orange-blossom water, cover the plate with foil or plastic wrap, and refrigerate for at least 2 hours, or until thoroughly chilled.

Just before serving, sprinkle the oranges with the confectioners' sugar and cinnamon. In Morocco, *lichine ma zhar* is served as a sweet "salad" course, but it may also be served as a dessert.

Flensjes *(Netherlands)*
PANCAKE CAKE

To serve 4

2¼ cups all-purpose flour
⅛ teaspoon salt
4 large eggs
1½ cups milk

4 tablespoons butter, melted
2 cups applesauce, or 1 cup
  applesauce and 1 cup cooked
  rhubarb

Sift the flour and salt into a deep mixing bowl, make a well in the center, and drop in the eggs. With a large spoon, gradually incorporate the flour and eggs. When they are thoroughly combined, pour in the milk in a thin stream, stirring constantly.

Place a small saucer about 6 inches in diameter, curved side up, in the center of a flat serving plate. (The saucer will prevent the completed pancakes from sagging in the middle.)

Heat a heavy 8-inch skillet (preferably one with a nonstick cooking surface) over moderate heat until a drop of water flicked into it steams for about 2 seconds before it evaporates. Brush the skillet with 2 teaspoons of the melted butter. Then, with a small ladle, pour in about 2 tablespoons of the batter, tipping the pan from side to side to spread it evenly over the whole surface of the pan. Cook the pancake for a minute or so, until a rim of brown shows around the edges, turn it over with a spatula, and cook the other side for a minute longer. With a large spatula, lift up the pancake and place it on top of the overturned saucer. Spread the top with 3 or 4 tablespoons of applesauce. Brush the skillet with another 1 or 2 teaspoons of melted butter, and cook another pancake as you did the first. Set the second cake on top of the first and spread it with more applesauce, or with 3 or 4 tablespoons of the rhubarb. Proceed with the remaining pancakes (there should be 8 or 9 in all), adding butter to the pan for each one and spreading the cakes with applesauce or alternating layers of applesauce and rhubarb as they are finished.

Slice the cake into pie-shaped wedges and serve at once.

Appelpannekoeken (*Netherlands*)
APPLE PANCAKES

To make 4 large pancakes

	pound stick)
2 cups all-purpose flour	2 medium-sized tart cooking apples,
½ teaspoon salt	peeled, quartered, cored and cut
4 large eggs, lightly beaten	lengthwise into ¼-inch-thick
2 cups milk	slices
12 tablespoons butter (1 quarter-	Golden or maple syrup

Combine the flour and salt in a deep bowl, make a well in the center, and pour in the eggs. With a large spoon or whisk, gradually incorporate the flour into the eggs. Then, stirring constantly, pour in the milk in a thin stream and continue to mix until the batter is smooth. Do not overmix.

In a heavy 8- to 9-inch skillet (preferably one with a nonstick cooking surface), melt 2 tablespoons of the butter over moderate heat. When the foam begins to subside, add about one fourth of the apple slices to the pan and turn them about in the butter until the slices are lightly and evenly browned. Pour in 1 cup of the batter and cook the pancake for 2 to 3 minutes. When it is browned around the edges, place a flat plate over the pan and invert the pancake onto the plate, browned side up. Add 1 tablespoon of butter to the pan and slide the pancake back for 2 minutes longer to brown the under side. Then slide it out of the skillet onto a heated plate. With a fork, roll the pancake into a cylinder and drape foil over it to keep it warm while you fry the remaining pancakes in the same way, using one fourth of the apple slices and 1 cup of batter for each one. Serve the pancakes as soon as possible after they are done, accompanied by the syrup presented in a sauceboat or pitcher.

NOTE: To prepare *spek pannekoeken,* or bacon pancakes, fry 8 slices of bacon in a 12-inch skillet until they are brown and barely crisp. Drain the bacon on paper towels and pour the fat into a measuring cup. For each cake, heat 2 tablespoons of the fat in an 8- to 9-inch skillet. Add 2 slices of the bacon to the skillet and pour in 1 cup of the batter. Fry as described above, using 2 slices of bacon and 1 cup of batter for each pancake, and adding fat to the skillet as needed.

Roomborstplaat *(Netherlands)*
COCOA-FLAVORED BROWN-SUGAR CANDY

To make about 1½ pounds

2 ounces shelled hazelnuts or walnuts	1½ cups superfine sugar
3 tablespoons butter, softened	1 cup dark-brown sugar
½ cup light cream	2 tablespoons unsweetened cocoa, preferably imported Dutch cocoa

Preheat the oven to 350°. Drop the nuts into enough boiling water to cover them completely and boil briskly for 2 minutes. Drain the nuts in a sieve, and with a small, sharp knife peel them while they are still hot. Spread the blanched nuts in a shallow baking dish and, turning them occasionally, toast them in the middle of the oven for about 5 minutes, or until they are delicately browned. Chop the hazelnuts or walnuts coarsely and set them aside.

With a pastry brush, spread 2 tablespoons of the softened butter evenly over the bottom and sides of a false-bottomed cake pan 8 inches in diameter and at least 2 inches deep. In a heavy enameled or stainless-steel saucepan, heat the cream and the remaining tablespoon of butter over moderate heat until the butter is dissolved and small bubbles appear around the edge of the pan. Reduce the heat to low and, stirring constantly, gradually add the superfine sugar, brown sugar, and cocoa. Continue to stir until the sugar and cocoa dissolve completely, then raise the heat to moderately low and cook undisturbed for about 15 minutes, or until the syrup reaches a temperature of 300° on a candy thermometer. (If you do not have a thermometer, drop a little of the syrup into a cup of ice water; when it reaches the proper temperature—or hard-crack stage —it should immediately form hard, brittle threads.)

Immediately remove the syrup from the heat, stir in the reserved nuts and pour the mixture into the buttered pan, smoothing it evenly with a spatula. Set aside at room temperature for about 1 hour, or until the candy is firm. To remove the *roomborstplaat* from the pan, set the pan on a large jar or coffee can and slip down the outside rim. Run a long metal spatula under the bottom of the candy to loosen it, then slide it out onto a plate. The candy is never cut, but is broken with the hands into irregularly shaped pieces. Although best if eaten the same day, the candy may be stored in airtight containers for 2 to 3 days.

Tmar Mihchi (*Tunisia*)
PISTACHIO-FILLED CANDIED DATES

To make about 4 dozen

	Glossary)
½ pound unsalted shelled pistachios	1 pound pitted dates
	2 cups water
3¾ cups sugar	A pinch of cream of tartar
2 tablespoons rose water (*see*	1 cup coarse white decorating sugar

Preheat the oven to 350°. Drop the pistachios into enough boiling water to cover them by at least 1 inch and boil briskly for 2 minutes. Drain at once and slip off the skins while the nuts are still hot. Spread the pistachios in a shallow baking pan and, turning occasionally, toast them in the middle of the oven for 8 to 10 minutes, until lightly colored.

Combine the pistachios and ¾ cup of the sugar in an electric blender and blend at high speed for 30 seconds. Turn off the machine, scrape down the sides of the jar with a rubber spatula and blend again until the nuts are pulverized. With the back of a spoon, rub the mixture through a fine sieve into a bowl. Add the rose water and beat vigorously to make a smooth paste.

With a small, sharp knife, cut a slit about 1 inch long and ½ inch deep in the side of each date. Stuff a rounded ½ teaspoon of the pistachio paste into the slit in each date and pinch the edges of the opening together firmly to enclose the filling.

Combine the water, the remaining 3 cups of sugar and the cream of tartar in a small saucepan and, stirring constantly, bring to a boil over moderate heat. Raise the heat to high and cook briskly, uncovered and undisturbed, until the syrup reaches a temperature of 230° on a candy thermometer, or until a few drops spooned into ice water immediately form coarse threads. Remove the pan from the heat.

Place the decorating sugar in a small bowl and lay several strips of wax paper beside it. Impale a date on a small skewer and immerse it in the syrup. Let the excess syrup drip off into the saucepan, then if you wish dip the date into the bowl of sugar to coat the surface lightly. Slide the date off the skewer onto the wax paper and candy the remaining dates.

Spread a fresh piece of wax paper in a deep serving dish and arrange the dates in rows on the paper. If necessary, cover the first layer of dates with another piece of wax paper and arrange the rest of the dates on top. Cover the top of the dish with wax paper and set the dates aside at room temperature for about 24 hours before serving.

Yo-yo *(Tunisia)*
ORANGE-FLAVORED DOUGHNUTS DIPPED IN HONEY SYRUP

To make 10 doughnuts

2 large eggs
¼ cup vegetable oil, plus vegetable
   oil for deep frying
¼ cup strained fresh orange juice
2 teaspoons finely grated orange
   peel
2¼ cups sugar
2 to 3 cups all-purpose flour
1 tablespoon baking soda
2 cups cold water
2 tablespoons strained fresh lemon
   juice
½ cup honey

In a deep bowl, combine the eggs, ¼ cup vegetable oil, orange juice, 1 teaspoon of the orange peel and ¼ cup of sugar. Beat vigorously with a wire whisk or spoon until the mixture is smooth. Then, beating constantly with a spoon, sift in 2 cups of the flour and the tablespoon of baking soda, and continue to beat until the mixture is thick enough to fall from the spoon in a wide, slowly dissolving ribbon.

Cover the bowl with a towel and set the dough aside to rest for at least 30 minutes.

Meanwhile prepare the syrup in the following fashion: In a small, heavy saucepan, bring the remaining 2 cups of sugar, the water and lemon juice to a boil over high heat, stirring until the sugar dissolves. Cook briskly, uncovered and undisturbed, until the syrup reaches a temperature of 230° on a candy thermometer. Reduce the heat to low, add the ½ cup honey and the remaining teaspoon of orange peel and simmer for 5 minutes. Then remove the pan from the heat and cover to keep the syrup warm.

Pour vegetable oil into a deep fryer or large, heavy saucepan to a depth of 3 inches and heat until the oil reaches a temperature of 350° on a deep-frying thermometer.

Flouring your hands heavily, gather the dough into a ball and divide it into 10 equal parts. Shape each part into a 2-inch round ball, then flatten it slightly. Hold the round in the palm of one hand and punch a hole through the center with the floured index finger of your other hand *(above)*.

Deep-fry the doughnuts, two or three at a time, for about 5 minutes, turning them about with a slotted spoon until they are golden brown on both sides. Transfer them to paper towels to drain, and fry and drain the remaining doughnuts similarly.

While the doughnuts are still warm, prick them in two or three places with the tines of a table fork. Then pick them up with tongs, dip them into the warm syrup, and serve at once.

Oliebollen *(Netherlands)*
NEW YEAR'S EVE FRITTERS

To make about 18 fritters

	Vegetable oil for deep frying
1 package active dry yeast	¼ cup dried currants
2 tablespoons sugar	¼ cup seedless raisins
1½ cups lukewarm (110° to	¼ cup coarsely chopped candied
115°) milk	orange peel
2 to 2½ cups all-purpose flour	2 tablespoons finely grated fresh
½ teaspoon salt	lemon peel
2 eggs	Confectioners' sugar

In a small bowl, sprinkle the yeast and a pinch of the sugar over the lukewarm milk. Let the mixture stand for 2 or 3 minutes, then stir to dissolve the yeast. Set the bowl in a warm, draft-free place such as an unlighted oven for about 5 minutes, or until the yeast bubbles up and the mixture almost doubles in volume.

Sift 2 cups of flour, the remaining sugar and the salt into a deep mixing bowl. Make a well in the center, pour in the yeast-and-milk mixture, and with a large spoon gradually incorporate the flour into the liquid ingredients. Drop in the eggs and beat until all of the flour has been absorbed. The dough should hold its shape lightly in the spoon; if the dough is too fluid, beat in up to ½ cup more flour, a few tablespoons at a time. Cover the bowl with a dampened kitchen towel and set it aside in the draft-free spot for about 1 hour, or until it doubles in bulk.

Pour vegetable oil into a deep fryer or large, heavy saucepan to a depth of about 3 inches and heat the oil until it reaches a temperature of 345° on a deep-frying thermometer.

Punch the dough down with a blow of your fist and gently but thoroughly stir in the currants, raisins, orange peel and lemon peel. For each of the *oliebollen,* scoop up about ¼ cup of the dough and drop it into the hot oil. Deep-fry 3 or 4 balls at a time, turning them with a slotted spoon, for about 10 minutes. As they brown, transfer the *oliebollen* to paper towels to drain.

Serve the *oliebollen* warm or at room temperature; they will stay crisp for 2 to 3 hours. Just before serving, dust the balls lightly with confectioners' sugar.

Pączki *(Poland)*
CARNIVAL JELLY DOUGHNUTS

To make about 2 dozen doughnuts

1 cup lukewarm milk (110° to 115°)
2 packages active dry yeast
⅔ cup confectioners' sugar
4 cups all-purpose flour
9 egg yolks
3 tablespoons rum
3 tablespoons vodka
½ teaspoon vanilla extract

1 teaspoon finely grated fresh
   orange peel
1 teaspoon finely grated fresh lemon
   peel
8 tablespoons (1 quarter-pound
   stick) unsalted butter, softened
¼ cup raspberry, cherry or
   blackberry preserves
Vegetable oil for deep frying

Pour the milk into a small bowl and sprinkle it with the yeast and ½ teaspoon of the confectioners' sugar. Let the mixture stand for 2 or 3 minutes, then stir to dissolve the yeast completely. Set the bowl aside in a warm, draft-free place (such as an unlighted oven) for about 10 minutes, or until the mixture almost doubles in volume.

Sift the flour and the remaining confectioners' sugar into a deep bowl and make a well in the center. Pour in the yeast mixture, egg yolks, rum, vodka and vanilla and, with a large spoon, gradually stir the flour into the liquid ingredients. Continue to stir until well mixed, then add the orange and lemon peel and beat in the softened butter, a few tablespoons at a time. The dough should be just firm enough to be gathered into a medium-soft ball.

On a lightly floured surface, knead the dough by pushing it down with the heels of your hands, pressing it forward and folding it back on itself. Repeat—pushing, pressing and folding—until the dough is smooth and elastic. Gather it into a ball, place it in a lightly buttered bowl, and dust the top with flour. Drape the bowl with a towel and set it aside in the draft-free place for about 1 hour, or until the dough doubles in volume.

Punch the dough down with a single blow of your fist and, on a lightly floured surface, roll it out into a rough circle about ½ inch thick. With a cookie cutter or the rim of a glass, cut the dough into 2½-inch rounds. Gather the scraps into a ball, roll it again to a thickness of ½ inch and cut out similar rounds of dough. You should have about 2 dozen rounds.

With your thumb, make a 1-inch round indentation in the center of each circle and fill it with about ½ teaspoon of the preserves. Lift up the edges of the dough around the filling and pinch the ends together to enclose the filling securely. Cover a baking sheet with a sheet of wax paper and place on it the doughnuts, seam side down and about 2 inches apart. Set aside in the draft-free place again for about 1 hour, or until the doughnuts have puffed up and doubled in size.

Pour the oil into a deep fryer or large heavy saucepan to a depth of 3 inches and heat until it reaches a temperature of 325° on a deep-frying thermometer. To deep-fry the doughnuts, lower 3 of them into the hot oil with a slotted spoon and fry for 4 minutes. Turn the doughnuts over with the spoon and continue to deep-fry uncovered for about 4 minutes longer, or until they are golden brown. Transfer them to drain on a platter lined with paper towels and fry the remaining doughnuts similarly.

Let the doughnuts cool to room temperature, then sprinkle them lightly with a little confectioners' sugar and serve.

Appelbeignets (*Netherlands*)
APPLE FRITTERS

To make about 24 fritters

BATTER	1 pint (2 cups) beer, at room
2 cups sifted all-purpose flour	temperature

Sift the flour into a deep mixing bowl and make a well in the center. Slowly pour in the beer and, stirring gently, gradually incorporate the flour. Continue to stir until the mixture is smooth, but do not beat or overmix. Set the batter aside to rest at room temperature for 3 hours before using.

APPLES	1 tablespoon ground cinnamon
5 medium-sized tart cooking apples	Vegetable oil for deep frying
1 cup sugar	Confectioners' sugar

Fifteen minutes or so before you plan to make the fritters, peel and core the apples and cut them crosswise into ⅓-inch-thick rounds. Lay the rounds side by side on a strip of wax paper. Then combine the sugar and cinnamon in a small bowl and sprinkle the mixture evenly over both sides of each apple round.

Preheat the oven to its lowest setting. Line a large shallow baking dish or jelly-roll pan with a double thickness of paper towels and set it in the middle of the oven. Pour vegetable oil into a deep fryer or large heavy saucepan to a depth of about 3 inches and heat the oil until it reaches a temperature of 375° on a deep-frying thermometer.

One at a time, pick up an apple slice with tongs or a slotted spoon, immerse it in the batter and, when it is well coated on all sides, drop it into the hot oil. Deep-fry 3 or 4 fritters at a time for about 4 minutes, turning them occasionally, until they are delicately and evenly browned. As they brown, transfer the fritters to the paper-lined pan and keep them warm in the oven while you coat and deep-fry the remaining apples.

Arrange the fritters on a heated platter and sprinkle them lightly with confectioners' sugar just before serving.

Alivenci (*Romania*)
CHEESE-AND-SOUR-CREAM SOUFFLÉ

To serve 4 to 6

1 tablespoon butter, softened	3 eggs
3 tablespoons flour	½ cup milk
8 ounces pot cheese	½ teaspoon salt
½ cup sour cream	Confectioners' sugar

Preheat the oven to 350°. With a pastry brush, spread the tablespoon of softened butter over the bottom and sides of an 8-inch-square baking dish at least 1½ inches deep. Add 2 tablespoons of the flour and tip the dish back and forth to spread it evenly. Invert the dish and rap it on a table to remove the excess flour. Set aside.

Force the pot cheese through a food mill into a deep bowl, or rub it through a fine sieve with the back of a spoon. Stir in the sour cream with a whisk or large spoon, then beat in the eggs, one at a time. Add the milk and salt, and the remaining 1 tablespoon of flour and continue to beat until the flour is completely absorbed.

Pour the soufflé into the baking dish and bake in the middle of the oven for about 30 minutes, or until the top puffs and is lightly browned. Sprinkle lightly with confectioners' sugar and serve at once.

Satou (*Romania*)
FROTHY WINE DESSERT

To serve 4

	1 cup white muscatel or other sweet
5 egg yolks	white wine
½ cup sugar	2 tablespoons fresh or frozen
1 tablespoon finely grated fresh	raspberries thoroughly defrosted
lemon peel	and drained (optional)

Place the egg yolks, sugar and lemon peel in the top of an enameled or stainless-steel double boiler set over barely simmering water. Beat with a whisk or a rotary beater or an electric hand mixer for 15 to 20 minutes, or until the mixture becomes a thick custard. In a separate pan, quickly bring the wine to a boil. Then pour it into the custard in a slow thin stream, beating all the while. Continue beating for another 10 minutes or so, until the *satou* is thick enough to coat a spoon heavily.

Spoon the *satou* into 4 individual dessert dishes or stemmed glasses and serve at once, while hot. If you like, you may rub 2 tablespoons of raspberries through a fine sieve with the back of a spoon and fold the purée into the *satou* just before serving.

Gaufres Bruxelloises (Belgium)
BRUSSELS-STYLE WAFFLES

To make about 6 waffles

1 package active dry yeast	7 tablespoons unsalted butter,
¼ cup sugar	melted and cooled
2½ cups lukewarm milk (110° to	2 egg whites
115°)	Confectioners' sugar
3 cups all-purpose flour	1 cup heavy cream, chilled and
⅛ teaspoon salt	whipped
2 egg yolks	1 pint fresh strawberries, washed
1 teaspoon vanilla extract	and hulled

In a small bowl sprinkle the yeast and a pinch of sugar over ½ cup of the lukewarm milk. Let the mixture stand for 2 or 3 minutes, then stir to blend the yeast and milk thoroughly. Set the bowl in a warm, draft-free place such as an unlighted oven for about 5 minutes, or until the yeast bubbles up and the mixture almost doubles in volume.

Sift the flour, the remaining sugar and the salt into a deep mixing bowl. Pour in the yeast mixture and the remaining 2 cups of lukewarm milk, and with a large spoon stir until the batter is smooth. Then thoroughly stir in the egg yolks, vanilla and the butter. Cover the bowl loosely with a kitchen towel and set it aside to rest in the warm, draft-free place for 30 minutes.

Following the manufacturers' directions, preheat a waffle iron (approximately 6 by 11 inches) to moderate. With a wire whisk or a rotary or electric beater, beat the egg whites until they are stiff enough to stand in unwavering peaks on the beater when it is lifted from the bowl. Stir the batter with a rubber spatula, add the egg whites and fold them into the batter gently but thoroughly.

Pour 1½ cups of the batter into the center of the hot waffle iron. Reduce the heat to moderately low, close the iron, and bake for 5 minutes, or until the steaming stops and the waffle is golden brown on both sides. (You can peek at the waffle to check its color after 3 minutes or so, but do not open the cover earlier or the waffle may stick to the grid.)

Serve at once, sprinkled with confectioners' sugar and accompanied by separate bowls of whipped cream and strawberries.

M'hannsha *(Morocco)*
PASTRY COILS FILLED WITH ALMOND PASTE ("THE SNAKE")

To make 12 small pastries

6 sheets *filo* pastry, each about 16 inches long and 12 inches wide, thoroughly defrosted if frozen *(see Glossary)*

8 tablespoons (1 quarter-pound stick) unsalted butter, melted,

plus 4 to 8 tablespoons butter
1 recipe for almond-paste filling *(page 144)*
2 to 4 tablespoons vegetable oil
¼ cup sugar mixed with ¼ teaspoon ground cinnamon

With a pastry wheel or sharp knife, cut each *filo* sheet in half crosswise to make a dozen 8-by-12-inch rectangles. For each *m'hannsha,* brush the entire top of one *filo* rectangle lightly with melted butter, then fold the *filo* in half to make a two-layered rectangle 8 inches long and 6 inches wide. Brush again with melted butter.

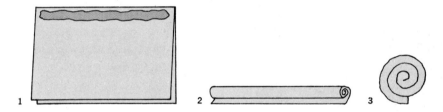

Spoon the almond paste into a pastry bag fitted with a ¼-inch plain tip and pipe the paste along the 8-inch side of the rectangle about ½ inch from the edge and to within about 1 inch of each end *(above, 1).* Turn the edge of the *filo* over the almond paste and roll the rectangle into a tight cylinder *(2),* tucking in the ends as you proceed. Brush the cylinder with a little butter and shape it into a coil *(3).*

When all of the *m'hannsha* have been filled and shaped, melt 2 tablespoon of butter with 1 tablespoon of oil in a heavy 10- to 12-inch skillet. When the foam begins to subside, add 2 of the *m'hannsha* and brown them in the hot fat, turning them over gently with a wide metal spatula and regulating the heat so that they color richly and evenly without burning. Transfer the browned pastries to a plate and sprinkle them with a little of the sugar-and-cinnamon mixture. Brown the remaining *m'hannsha* in the same fashion, adding butter and oil to the skillet as needed. Serve the pastries warm or at room temperature.

Cakes, Pies and Cookies

Makroud el Louse (Algeria)
SOFT ALMOND COOKIES

To make about 6 dozen cookies

2½ pounds blanched whole
   almonds, finely pulverized in a
   nut grinder or with a mortar and
   pestle (6 cups)
2½ cups sugar

2 tablespoons finely grated lemon peel
4 eggs
2 cups cold water
1 tablespoon orange-blossom water
   (see Glossary)
4 cups confectioners' sugar

Preheat the oven to 350°. In a deep bowl, stir the almonds, 2 cups of the sugar and the lemon peel together until they are well blended. Make a well in the center, drop in the eggs and, with a wooden spoon, slowly stir the ingredients together. Continue to stir until the mixture is smooth.

Divide the mixture into quarters. On a heavily floured surface, roll each quarter with the palms of your hands into a cylinder about 18 inches long and 1½ inches in diameter. Flour your hands constantly as you roll the dough to prevent it from sticking to your fingers.

Flatten each cylinder into an oblong about 2 inches wide and, holding a sharp knife at a 45-degree angle, cut each cylinder diagonally into 1½-inch-thick slices. Dust the slices with flour, place them about 1 inch apart on ungreased baking sheets, and bake in the middle of the oven for about 15 minutes, or until the cookies just begin to color. Dust off any excess flour with a pastry brush and transfer the cookies to wire racks to cool.

Meanwhile, prepare the syrup in the following fashion: Combine the remaining ½ cup of sugar and the water in a small saucepan and bring to a boil over high heat, stirring with a wooden spoon until the sugar dissolves. Cook briskly, uncovered and undisturbed, for 15 minutes. Pour the syrup into a shallow bowl and when it has cooled to room temperature, stir in the tablespoon of orange-blossom water.

Spread the confectioners' sugar in a large shallow pan or on paper towels. Dip the cookies one at a time into the syrup and, when they are coated on both sides, roll them in the confectioners' sugar. Set the cookies aside on paper towels to dry. In tightly covered jars or tins, the cookies can be kept for several months.

Speculaasjes *(Netherlands)*

SAINT NICHOLAS SPICE COOKIES

To make 2 large figures plus 2 dozen cookies, or to make 6 dozen cookies

2 tablespoons butter, softened, plus 12 tablespoons butter (1½ quarter-pound sticks), softened
2 to 2¼ cups all-purpose flour
1 tablespoon ground cinnamon
½ teaspoon ground mace
½ teaspoon ground anise, or ½ teaspoon anise seeds pulverized with a mortar and pestle or in a small bowl with the back of a spoon
¼ teaspoon ground ginger

¼ teaspoon ground nutmeg
¼ teaspoon ground cloves
¼ teaspoon double-acting baking powder
⅛ teaspoon salt
1 cup light- or dark-brown sugar
3 tablespoons milk
24 blanched whole almonds, split into halves
1 cup slivered blanched almonds plus ½ cup sliced almonds

NOTE: If you are making 6 dozen cookies, omit the whole and slivered almonds and use 1½ cups sliced almonds.

Preheat the oven to 375°. With a pastry brush, spread 2 tablespoons of the softened butter evenly on two large baking sheets. Combine 2 cups of the flour, the cinnamon, mace, anise, ginger, nutmeg, cloves, baking powder and salt, and sift them together into a bowl. Set aside.

In a deep bowl, cream the remaining 12 tablespoons of butter and the sugar together by beating and mashing them against the sides of the bowl with a large spoon until light and fluffy. Beat in the milk a tablespoon at a time, then add the flour-and-spice mixture about ½ cup at a time, beating well after each addition. When finished the dough should be firm enough to gather into a compact ball; if necessary, add up to ¼ cup more flour by the tablespoonful. Should the dough become too stiff to beat easily, knead in the remaining flour with your hands.

If you plan to make figures, cut the dough in half and roll out each

half of the dough between sheets of lightly floured wax paper, making two rectangles, each about 9 inches wide, 12 inches long and ¼ inch thick. Remove the top sheets of wax paper and, lifting up the bottom sheets, invert the dough onto the baking sheets and peel off the wax paper. Following the photograph at left, cut out two figures with the point of a sharp knife. Gently pull away the excess dough and set it aside to make rectangular cookies as described below. Decorate the figures with the point of the knife and with the halved and slivered almonds, as shown in the photograph.

To make small rectangular cookies of the excess dough (or to make small cookies of all of the dough), roll out the dough between two sheets of wax paper until it is about ⅟₁₆ inch thick. Gently pull away the top sheet of wax paper and, with a pastry wheel or sharp knife, cut the dough into 1½-by-2½-inch rectangles. Press the sliced almonds gently into the cookies, dividing the nuts evenly among them. Refrigerate the cookies for about 30 minutes, then transfer them from the bottom sheet of wax paper to the buttered baking sheets with a metal spatula.

Bake the figures in the middle of the oven for about 15 minutes, or until they are lightly browned and firm to the touch. The cookies will take only 8 to 10 minutes to brown and firm. Let the figures and cookies cool to room temperature before removing them from the baking sheets. Stored in airtight containers, the cookies will keep for several weeks.

Medeni Kurabii *(Bulgaria)*
HONEY COOKIES

To make about 2 dozen cookies

8 tablespoons unsalted butter (1 quarter-pound stick, melted but not browned, and cooled	1 teaspoon baking soda
	1 egg yolk
	1 cup all-purpose flour
¼ cup honey	½ cup coarse white decorating
¼ cup sugar	sugar

Preheat the oven to 350°. In a deep bowl, combine the cooled butter, honey, sugar, soda and egg yolk, and beat vigorously with a wooden spoon until the ingredients are thoroughly mixed. Sift in the flour, a few tablespoons at a time, beating well after each addition. The dough should be just firm enough to be gathered into a soft but compact ball.

To shape each cookie, pinch off about 1 rounded teaspoon of dough and, on a heavily floured surface, roll it with the palm of your hand into a ball about 1 inch in diameter. Dip the top of the ball into the coarse sugar and place it sugared side up on a large ungreased baking sheet. Make similar balls of the remaining dough and arrange them about ½ inch apart on the baking sheet. Bake in the middle of the oven for about 10 minutes, or until the cookies are delicately browned. With a metal spatula, transfer the cookies to a wire cake rack to cool. Serve them at once or store them in a tightly covered jar or tin.

Gevulde Boterkoek *(Netherlands)*
BUTTER CAKE WITH ALMOND-PASTE FILLING

To make one 8-inch round cake

ALMOND FILLING
⅔ cup blanched almonds,
    pulverized in a blender or with a
    nut grinder and rubbed through
    a sieve

½ cup sugar
1 egg
⅓ cup seedless raisins
2 tablespoons orange marmalade
1 tablespoon finely grated lemon peel

Starting one or even two days ahead, prepare the almond filling. Combine the almonds, ½ cup of sugar and 1 egg in a bowl, and mix thoroughly. Stir in the raisins, marmalade and lemon peel, then cover the bowl with a dampened towel and set aside at room temperature for at least 24 hours and up to 48 hours.

BUTTER CAKE
½ pound plus 2 tablespoons
    unsalted butter, softened

1 cup sugar
1 egg

In a deep bowl, cream ½ pound of softened butter and 1 cup of sugar together by beating and mashing them against the sides of the bowl with a large spoon until light and fluffy. Beat in the egg, then add 2 cups of flour, about ½ cup at a time, stirring well after each addition. When finished, the dough should be firm enough to gather into a compact ball; if necessary, add up to ½ cup more flour by the tablespoon. Wrap the dough in wax paper and refrigerate it for about 20 minutes. Meanwhile, with a pastry brush, spread the remaining 2 tablespoons of softened butter evenly over the bottom and sides of an 8-inch round false-bottom cake pan 1½ inches deep.

Break off about half of the dough and, dipping your hands into the remaining ¼ cup of flour occasionally, shape the dough into a flattened round 7 or 8 inches in diameter. Place the round in the buttered pan and, with floured fingers, pat and smooth the dough until it completely and evenly covers the bottom of the pan. On a lightly floured surface pat and shape the remaining half of the dough into a cylinder about 12 inches long and 1 to 2 inches in diameter. Chill for another 20 minutes.

1 egg white, lightly beaten

2 to 2¾ cups all-purpose flour

Preheat the oven to 325°. With a spatula, smooth the almond-filling mixture evenly over the pastry in the pan. With a sharp knife, slice the cylinder crosswise into 1-inch-thick rounds. With the spatula, flatten the rounds further and arrange them on top of the filling, overlapping them slightly and pinching the edges together so that the pastry covers the filling completely. Brush the top with the beaten egg white and bake in the middle of the oven for about 1½ hours, or until golden brown.

Remove the pan from the oven, and set it on a large jar or coffee can and slip down the outside rim. Let it cool to room temperature, then run a long metal spatula under the cake to loosen it and slide it off onto a large serving plate.

Mazurek Wielkanocny *(Poland)*
FLAKY FINGER COOKIES TOPPED WITH ALMONDS

To make about 6 dozen cookies

PASTRY
2 cups plus 2 tablespoons all-
    purpose flour
2 cups confectioners' sugar

4 hard-cooked egg yolks
1 teaspoon vanilla extract
½ pound plus 1 tablespoon
    unsalted butter, softened

Sift 2 cups of flour and the confectioners' sugar into a deep mixing bowl. With the back of a spoon, rub the egg yolks through a fine sieve directly into the flour-and-sugar mixture. Stir until well combined, then add the vanilla and beat in ½ pound of butter a few tablespoons at a time. Continue to beat vigorously with the spoon, or knead with your hands, until the dough is smooth and can be gathered into a compact ball. Wrap in wax paper and refrigerate the dough for at least 1 hour.

Preheat the oven to 375°. With a pastry brush, spread a large baking sheet with the remaining tablespoon of softened butter. Sprinkle the 2 tablespoons of flour over the butter and tip the sheet from side to side to spread it evenly. Invert the sheet and rap the bottom sharply to remove the excess flour.

ALMOND TOPPING
1 egg, lightly beaten

4 ounces (1 cup) sliced blanched
    almonds

On a lightly floured surface, roll out the dough into a 12-inch square that is less than ¼ inch thick. Trim the edges to make a perfect square. Cut the dough into quarters and, with a long, wide metal spatula, carefully transfer the quarters to the baking sheet, placing them side by side in their original positions. Cover the dough with a sheet of lightly floured wax paper and gently roll the dough again to join the seams. Peel off the wax paper and brush the entire surface of the dough with the beaten egg.

Sprinkle the top of the dough evenly with the cup of sliced almonds, pressing them gently into the surface. Bake in the middle of the oven for 20 to 25 minutes, or until the pastry is golden brown. Remove the pan from the oven and, with a lightly buttered knife or pastry wheel, cut the pastry into strips about 2 inches long and 1 inch wide. With a metal spatula carefully transfer the *mazurek* to a wire cake rack and let them cool to room temperature.

In a tightly covered container, the cookies may safely be kept for as long as 2 to 3 weeks.

Zuger Kirschtorte *(Switzerland)*
CHERRY-BRANDY CAKE

To make one 9-inch cake

MERINGUE
2 tablespoons butter, softened
2 tablespoons flour
3 egg whites

⅛ teaspoon cream of tartar
1 cup sugar
1 cup ground hazelnuts, pulverized
    with a nut grinder or in a blender

To make the meringues: Preheat the oven to 250°. With a pastry brush, spread the softened butter on two large baking sheets. Sprinkle the sheets with the 2 tablespoons of flour, tipping the sheets from side to side to spread it evenly. Then turn the sheets over and rap them sharply to remove the excess flour. Center an inverted 9-inch plate or layer-cake pan on the sheets one at a time and, with the tip of a knife or your finger, draw a 9-inch circle using the pan as a guide. Set the circled sheets aside.

In a deep unlined copper bowl (glass or stainless steel will do, but do not use aluminum), beat the egg whites and cream of tartar with a wire whisk or a rotary or electric beater for about a minute, or until they thicken slightly. Beating constantly, add 1 cup of the sugar a few tablespoons at a time and beat for at least 5 minutes. The meringue when finished should be stiff, glossy and stand in firm peaks. Add 1 cup of the ground nuts and with a rubber spatula fold them in gently but thoroughly.

With the spatula, smooth the meringue inside the two 9-inch circles on the baking sheets—dividing it between them to make layers about ¼ inch thick. Bake for 45 minutes in the middle of the oven, until the layers are firm and dry to the touch. Lower the oven heat if they begin to brown at any point. Remove the pans from the oven and run a long metal spatula under the bottom of the meringues to loosen them. Let them cool on the baking sheets.

GÉNOISE CAKE
2 teaspoons butter, softened
1 tablespoon flour
8 tablespoons unsalted butter, cut
    into ¼-inch bits

3 eggs
½ cup sugar
½ teaspoon vanilla extract
½ cup sifted all-purpose flour

To make the *Génoise* cake: Preheat the oven to 350°. With a pastry brush, spread the 2 teaspoons of softened butter evenly over the bottom and sides of a 9-inch round cake pan 1½ inches deep. Sprinkle the tablespoon of flour into the pan, tip it from side to side to spread the flour evenly, then invert the pan and rap it sharply on a table to remove any excess flour. Set the pan aside.

Clarify the 8 tablespoons of butter in a small saucepan by melting it slowly over low heat without letting the butter brown. Let it rest off the heat for a minute, then skim off the foam. Spoon the clear butter into a bowl and discard the milky solids at the bottom of the pan.

In an electric mixer, beat the eggs, ½ cup sugar and vanilla together at high speed for at least 15 minutes, or until the mixture is thick and fluffy and has almost tripled in volume. A little at a time, sift the ½ cup of flour over the eggs, folding it in gently with a rubber spatula. Finally, add the clarified butter 2 tablespoons at a time and continue to fold until all traces of the butter disappear. Do not overfold or the cake will be heavy instead of airy and light. Gently pour the batter into the prepared cake pan, spreading it and smoothing the top with the spatula.

Bake in the middle of the oven for 20 to 25 minutes, or until the cake puffs above the rim of the pan, shrinks slightly away from the sides and a cake tester inserted into the center comes out clean. Remove the cake from the oven and let it cool in the pan for about 5 minutes. Turn the cake out onto a rack to cool completely.

BUTTER CREAM

½ cup milk

A 2-inch piece of vanilla bean, split lengthwise in half, or substitute 1 teaspoon vanilla extract

4 egg yolks

½ cup sugar

½ pound unsalted butter, softened

1 tablespoon imported kirsch

4 to 5 drops red vegetable food coloring

To make the butter cream: In a 2- to 3-quart saucepan, heat the milk and the vanilla bean (if you are using it) over low heat until bubbles form around the edge of the pan. Remove the pan from the heat and set aside for 10 or 15 minutes.

Combine the egg yolks and ½ cup of sugar in a deep bowl and beat with a wire whisk or a rotary or electric beater for at least 5 minutes, or until the mixture is thick enough to fall in a slowly dissolving ribbon from the beater when it is lifted from the pan. Discard the vanilla bean and, beating constantly, slowly pour the milk into the egg yolks.

Return the mixture to the saucepan and, stirring with a wooden spoon, cook over low heat until the eggs are thick enough to coat the spoon heavily. Do not let the mixture (now a custard) come near a boil or it will curdle. Immediately place the pan in a large bowl or pot filled with crushed ice or ice cubes and water, and continue to stir until the custard has cooled to room temperature. Stir in the vanilla extract (if you are using it), then beat in the butter, 2 tablespoons at a time, and continue beating until the butter is completely absorbed. Then beat in 1 tablespoon of kirsch and slowly add enough of the red food coloring to the butter cream to tint it a pale pink. Cover the pan with wax paper and refrigerate the butter cream (there should be about 1 cup) for about 30 minutes, or until it has become firm enough to spread.

Continued on next page

SYRUP
¼ cup sugar

¼ cup water
2 teaspoons imported kirsch

Meanwhile, prepare the syrup: In a small saucepan, bring ¼ cup of sugar and the water to a boil over moderate heat, stirring until the sugar dissolves. Raise the heat to high and cook briskly, uncovered and undisturbed, for 5 minutes, or until the syrup reaches a temperature of 220° on a candy thermometer. Remove the pan from the heat.

With a long serrated knife, cut the cooled spongecake in half horizontally. Stir 2 teaspoons of kirsch into the syrup and dribble it as evenly as possible over the cut side of each cake half.

½ cup ground hazelnuts,
   pulverized with a nut grinder or

in a blender
½ cup confectioners' sugar

To assemble the cake: Place one meringue on a serving plate and, with a metal spatula, spread 2 tablespoons of the butter cream evenly over it. Top with a layer of the cake (moistened side up) and spread it with another 2 tablespoons of butter cream. Add the second cake layer, cover it with 2 tablespoons of butter cream, and then set the second meringue in place on top of the cake. Smooth the remaining 8 tablespoons of butter cream over the top and sides of the cake. Sprinkle the ½ cup of hazelnuts on the sides of the cake, patting them gently in place. Refrigerate the torte for 1 to 2 hours. Just before serving, sift the confectioners' sugar over the top.

Babka Wielkanocna (Poland)
EASTER CAKE WITH RAISINS

To make 1 large cake

CAKE

1¼ cups lukewarm milk (110° to 115°)
1 package active dry yeast
6 tablespoons sugar
2½ to 2¾ cups all-purpose flour
½ teaspoon salt
10 egg yolks

¾ pound plus 2 tablespoons unsalted butter, softened
1 cup white seedless raisins
2 tablespoons finely grated orange peel
1 tablespoon finely grated lemon peel

Pour the lukewarm milk into a small bowl and sprinkle it with the yeast and ½ teaspoon of the sugar. Let the mixture stand for 2 or 3 minutes, then stir to dissolve the yeast completely. Set the bowl aside in a warm, draft-free place (such as an unlighted oven) for about 10 minutes, or until the mixture almost doubles in volume.

Place 2½ cups of the flour, the remaining sugar and the salt in a deep mixing bowl and make a well in the center. Pour in the yeast mixture and the egg yolks and, with a large spoon, gradually stir the flour into the liquid ingredients. Continue to stir until well mixed, then beat in ¾ pound of butter a few tablespoonfuls at a time. The dough should be firm enough to be gathered into a medium-soft ball. If necessary, stir in up to ¼ cup more flour, adding it by the tablespoon.

Transfer the dough to an electric mixer equipped with a kneading hook and knead for about 20 minutes, or until the dough is very smooth, glossy and elastic. Or knead the dough by hand—pushing it down with the heels of your hands, pressing it forward and folding it back on itself —for about 40 minutes.

Shape the dough into a ball, place it in a lightly buttered bowl and dust the top with flour. Drape a towel over the bowl and set it aside in the draft-free place for about 1 hour, or until the dough doubles in volume. With a pastry brush, spread the 2 tablespoons of softened butter over the bottom and sides of a Turk head mold or, less traditionally, a 2-quart *Gugelhupf* pan. Sprinkle the butter with the remaining ¼ cup of flour and tip the pan from side to side to spread it evenly. Invert the pan and rap it sharply to remove the excess flour.

Punch the dough down with a single blow of your fist and into it knead the raisins, orange peel and lemon peel. Pat the dough evenly over the bottom of the buttered and floured mold, drape with a towel, and set aside in the draft-free place again for 1 hour, or until the dough has doubled in volume and risen almost to the top of the mold.

Preheat the oven to 375°. Bake the cake in the middle of the oven for about 40 minutes, or until it is golden brown. Turn the cake out onto a cake rack and let it cool briefly at room temperature while you prepare the icing.

WHITE ICING

2 cups confectioners' sugar
¼ cup cold water

2 teaspoons strained fresh lemon juice

In a small bowl, combine the confectioners' sugar, water and lemon juice, and beat vigorously together with a spoon until they are smooth. Pour the icing slowly over the top of the warm cake, allowing it to run down the sides. Let the *babka* cool to room temperature before serving.

Tort Orzechowy *(Poland)*
WALNUT LAYER CAKE WITH COFFEE-BUTTER ICING

To make one 9-inch round cake

TORTE
1 tablespoon butter, softened
2 tablespoons flour
10 egg whites
10 egg yolks

1½ cups confectioners' sugar
1 teaspoon vanilla extract
1 pound shelled walnuts (4 cups),
    finely grated in a nut grinder or
    pulverized with a mortar and
    pestle
4 tablespoons dry white bread crumbs

Preheat the oven to 350°. With a pastry brush, spread the tablespoon of softened butter over the bottom and sides of a 9-inch springform pan about 3 inches deep. Sprinkle the flour over the butter and tip the pan from side to side to spread it evenly. Invert the pan and rap it sharply on the bottom to remove the excess flour.

In a deep bowl, beat the egg whites with a wire whisk or a rotary or electric beater until they are stiff enough to stand in firm, unwavering peaks on the beater when it is lifted from the bowl. In another deep bowl, using the same unwashed beater, beat the egg yolks for 1 minute. Then, beating constantly, sift in 1½ cups of confectioners' sugar a little at a time, add the vanilla, and beat for 4 or 5 minutes, until the mixture is thick enough to fall in a slowly dissolving ribbon from the beater.

Scoop the egg whites over the egg-yolk mixture and, with a rubber spatula, fold them together, using an over-under cutting motion rather than a stirring motion. When no trace of white remains, gently but thoroughly fold in the pulverized nuts, ½ cup or so at a time. Then fold in the dry bread crumbs. Pour the batter into the buttered and floured pan, spreading it and smoothing the top with the spatula. Bake in the middle of the oven for about 1 hour, or until the torte has puffed and begun to pull slightly away from the sides of the pan. Turn off the oven, open the door and let the torte rest for 10 minutes. Then remove the sides of the pan, slide a thin knife under the bottom of the cake, and carefully slide it onto a wire cake rack to cool to room temperature.

ICING
1 pound unsalted butter, softened
1½ cups confectioners' sugar
2 egg yolks
2 tablespoons instant coffee,

dissolved in 3 tablespoons boiling
    water and cooled
6 ounces (1½ cups) shelled
    walnuts, coarsely chopped

Meanwhile, prepare the coffee-butter icing. In a large bowl, cream the pound of softened butter and 1½ cups of confectioners' sugar together, beating and mashing them against the sides of the bowl with a spoon until they are light and fluffy. Beat in 2 egg yolks, 1 at a time, and stir in the dissolved coffee. Continue to beat until the icing is creamy and thick, then refrigerate for about 15 minutes, or until it is firm enough to spread.

To assemble the torte, slice the cake horizontally into two layers with a long, sharp knife, preferably one with a serrated blade. Place the bottom slice cut side up on a serving plate and, with a metal spatula or knife, spread it with a ½-inch-thick layer of the icing. Set the second layer over it, cut side down, and spread the top and sides with the remaining icing. Gently press the chopped walnuts onto the top and sides of the cake and refrigerate until ready to serve.

Mazurek Czekoladowy *(Poland)*
FLAKY FINGER COOKIES WITH CHOCOLATE MERINGUE

To make about 6 dozen cookies

1 recipe for *mazurek* pastry *(page 131)*
8 egg whites
1 cup sugar
⅓ cup cold water
2 ounces bittersweet cooking chocolate, melted and cooled
⅓ cup sifted confectioners' sugar
4 ounces blanched toasted almonds, pulverized in a nut grinder or with a mortar and pestle
1 tablespoon finely grated fresh lemon peel

Prepare and roll out the *mazurek* pastry as described on page 131, then bake in a 375° oven for 10 minutes, or until the top is pale gold. Remove from the oven and cool to room temperature on the baking sheet.

Preheat the oven to 225°. In a deep bowl, beat the egg whites with a wire whisk or a rotary or electric beater until they are stiff enough to form unwavering peaks on the beater when it is lifted from the bowl.

In a small saucepan, bring the sugar and water to a boil over moderate heat, stirring until the sugar dissolves. Increase the heat to high and cook briskly, uncovered and undisturbed, until the syrup reaches a temperature of 220° on a candy thermometer, or until a few drops spooned into ice water immediately form a soft ball.

Beating constantly, pour the hot syrup in a thin stream into the egg whites and continue to beat until the meringue is smooth and thick. Still beating, pour in the melted, cooled chocolate and slowly add the confectioners' sugar. With a rubber spatula, gently but thoroughly fold in the almonds and the lemon peel. Spread the meringue evenly over the entire surface of the cooled pastry.

Bake in the middle of the oven for 1 hour, or until the meringue is dry. Remove the pan from the oven and, with a lightly buttered knife, cut the *mazurek czekoladowy* into strips about 2 inches long and 1 inch wide. With a metal spatula, carefully transfer the cookies to a wire cake rack and cool to room temperature before serving.

Engadiner Nusstorte *(Switzerland)*
WALNUT CAKE

To make one 9-inch cake

PASTRY
3 cups sifted all-purpose flour
¼ cup sugar
⅛ teaspoon salt
½ pound butter, chilled and cut
into ¼-inch bits
1 egg
2 teaspoons finely grated fresh
lemon peel
1 tablespoon dark rum

In a large, chilled bowl combine the flour, sugar, salt and butter. With your finger tips rub the flour and fat together until they look like flakes of coarse meal. Do not let the mixture become oily.

Mix the egg, lemon peel and rum together with a fork and pour them over the flour mixture all at once. Toss together lightly and gather the dough into a ball, kneading it with your hands until it forms a compact mass. Then dust it lightly with flour, wrap in wax paper, and refrigerate for at least 2 hours before using.

Preheat the oven to 350°. Break off about three quarters of the dough and, on a lightly floured surface, pat it into a rough circle about 1 inch thick. Dust a little flour over and under it and roll it out from the center to within an inch of the far edge of the pastry. Lift the dough and turn it clockwise about 2 inches; roll again from the center to within an inch or so of the far edge. Repeat—lifting, turning, rolling—until the circle is about ⅛ inch thick and 12 inches in diameter. If the dough sticks, lift it gently with a metal spatula and sprinkle a little flour under it.

Drape the dough over the rolling pin, lift it up, and unroll it slackly over a 9-inch springform pan. Gently press the dough into the bottom and around the sides of the pan, to make a shell 1 inch deep, being careful not to stretch it, or it will contract as it bakes.

Combine any scraps with the remaining piece of dough, gather into a ball and wrap in wax paper. Refrigerate it and the pastry-lined springform while you prepare the filling.

FILLING
1 cup heavy cream
1⅓ cups sugar
3 tablespoons honey
2 tablespoons imported kirsch
3 cups coarsely chopped walnuts

In a small pan heat the cream until small bubbles appear around the edge. Cover and set aside off the heat. Pour the sugar into a 2- to 3-quart saucepan, set it over moderate heat and, stirring constantly, let the sugar melt into a smooth syrup. Then, tipping the pan back and forth almost constantly, simmer the syrup until it turns a pale golden brown. Pour the reserved warm cream into the syrup in a slow thin stream, stirring constantly. When the mixture is smooth remove the pan from the heat and stir in the honey, kirsch and nuts.

1 egg combined with 2 tablespoons milk and beaten lightly

Pour the filling into the lined springform pan, spreading it and smoothing the top with a metal spatula. With a pastry brush, lightly coat the rim of the pastry with egg-and-milk mixture.

Roll out the ball of refrigerated dough into a rectangle about 5 inches wide and 10½ inches long. With a pastry wheel or sharp knife, cut the rectangle into 10 strips about ½ inch wide. Cover the filling with a crisscrossing lattice of the pastry strips. Trim off the excess dough and pinch the ends of the lattice strips to secure them to the moistened rim.

Brush the lattice with the remaining egg-and-milk mixture. Then bake the torte in the middle of the oven for 40 to 45 minutes, or until the filling is firm and the crust is crisp and golden. Remove the torte from the oven and cool to room temperature before removing the sides of the pan. Cut the torte into wedges and serve it accompanied, if you like, by a bowl of unsweetened whipped cream.

Masni Kurabii (Bulgaria)
LARD-AND-YOGHURT COOKIES

To make about 4 dozen cookies

½ cup lard, melted and cooled	¾ cup finely ground walnuts,
½ cup unflavored yoghurt	pulverized in a blender or with a
½ cup sugar	nut grinder or mortar and pestle
¼ teaspoon baking soda	2 to 2¼ cups all purpose flour
1 egg yolk	¼ cup confectioners' sugar

Preheat the oven to 350°. In a deep bowl, combine the melted and cooled lard, the yoghurt, sugar, baking soda and egg yolk. Beat vigorously with a wooden spoon until the ingredients are well mixed. Stir in the walnuts, then sift in 2 cups of the flour, about ¼ cup at a time, beating well after each addition. The dough should be just firm enough to be gathered into a compact ball. If it is too soft beat in up to ¼ cup more of flour a tablespoon at a time.

To shape each cookie, pinch off 1 rounded teaspoon of dough and, on a heavily floured surface, with the palm of your hand, roll it into a ball about 1 inch in diameter. Arrange the cookies about 1 inch apart on two large ungreased baking sheets. Bake in the middle of the oven for about 25 minutes, or until the cookies are delicately browned. With a metal spatula, transfer the cookies to wire cake racks to cool. Sprinkle lightly with the confectioners' sugar just before serving. The lard cookies will keep at least a week if stored in tightly covered containers.

Samsa *(Tunisia)*
ALMOND-AND-SESAME-SEED PASTRY

To make about 2 dozen pastries

2¾ cups (1 pound) blanched slivered almonds

1 pound (about 3 cups) white sesame seeds

1¼ pounds unsalted butter, melted and cooled

20 sheets *filo* pastry, each about 16 inches long and 12 inches wide,

thoroughly defrosted if frozen *(see Glossary)*

1 cup sugar

1 cup water

2 tablespoons strained fresh lemon juice

1 tablespoon rose water *(see Glossary)*

Preheat the oven to 350°. Spread the almonds and sesame seeds evenly in a large shallow baking pan and brown them in the middle of the oven for about 10 minutes, stirring them from time to time so that they color evenly. A cup or so at a time, pulverize the almonds and sesame seeds in the jar of an electric blender. As they are pulverized, scrape the mixture into a deep bowl with a rubber spatula.

With a pastry brush, spread about 1 tablespoon of the melted butter over the bottom and sides of a 12-by-8-by-2-inch baking dish. Brush a sheet of *filo* pastry generously with butter and fold it in half making a 12-by-8-inch rectangle. Fit it into the dish and smooth out the pastry. Brush the top with butter and repeat with 4 more sheets of *filo,* buttering them, folding them, and placing one upon the other.

Spread the top sheet of *filo* evenly with 1 cup of almond-and-sesame-seed mixture, then add 5 sheets of *filo* as before. Spread another cup of the almonds and seeds over the pastry and cover with 5 more buttered and folded sheets of *filo.*

Spread any remaining almonds and sesame seeds over the top. Then cover them with the remaining 5 sheets of *filo,* buttering and folding the pastry as before. Brush the top with melted butter and, with a sharp knife, cut the pastry into 2-inch squares.

Bake the *samsa* in the middle of the oven for 30 minutes, lower the temperature to 300°, and bake for 30 minutes longer, or until the top is crisp and golden brown.

Meanwhile prepare the syrup in the following fashion: Combine the sugar and water in a small saucepan and bring to a boil over moderate heat, stirring until the sugar dissolves. Increase the heat to high and boil briskly, uncovered, for about 5 minutes, or until the syrup reaches a temperature of 220° on a candy thermometer. Pour the syrup into a bowl or pitcher and stir in the lemon juice and rose water. Cool the syrup to room temperature before using it.

When the pastry is done, and while it is still hot, pour the syrup evenly over the top. Cool to room temperature before serving.

Aargauer Rüeblitorte *(Switzerland)*
CARROT-AND-ALMOND CAKE

To make one 10-inch round cake

1 tablespoon butter, softened
1 cup dried bread crumbs
1½ cups blanched almonds,
    pulverized in a blender or nut
    grinder and then shaken through
    a fine sieve
¾ cup finely grated scraped carrots
1 tablespoon finely grated fresh
    lemon peel
1 teaspoon ground ginger

½ teaspoon ground mace
½ teaspoon ground cinnamon
5 egg whites
5 egg yolks
1¼ cups sugar
1 tablespoon double-acting baking
    powder
¼ cup imported kirsch
5 tablespoons confectioners' sugar
    combined with 2 teaspoons cold
    water

Preheat the oven to 350°. With a pastry brush, spread the softened butter over the bottom and sides of a 10-inch springform cake pan. Drop in the bread crumbs, tipping the pan to coat the bottom and sides evenly. Invert the pan and rap it gently to remove the excess crumbs.

In a mixing bowl, combine the almonds, carrots, lemon peel, ginger, mace and cinnamon, and mix well. Set aside.

In a deep bowl, preferably of unlined copper (glass or stainless steel will do if necessary, but definitely not aluminum), beat the egg whites with a whisk or a rotary or electric beater until they are stiff enough to stand in unwavering peaks when the beater is lifted from the bowl.

In another bowl and with the same beater, beat the egg yolks for 30 seconds or so. Then slowly sift in the sugar and continue beating for 3 or 4 minutes, until the yolks are very thick. With a wooden spoon, stir in the baking powder and kirsch, then mix in the reserved almond-and-carrot mixture about ½ cup at a time.

Vigorously stir about a quarter of the egg whites into the batter to lighten it. Spoon the remaining egg whites over the batter and, with a rubber spatula, fold them gently together, continuing to fold until no streaks of white show. Do not overfold.

Ladle the batter into the cake pan, spreading it out and smoothing the top with the spatula. Bake in the middle of the oven for 1 hour, or until a cake tester inserted in the center of the cake comes out clean. Let the cake cool for about 5 minutes before removing the sides of the pan. Then, inserting a large spatula under the cake, slide it onto a wire rack. While the cake is still warm, brush the top with the confectioners' sugar mixture to glaze it lightly.

Let the cake cool to room temperature before serving.

Apfelwähe *(Switzerland)*
APPLE TART WITH APRICOT PRESERVES

To make one 9-inch tart

4 medium-sized tart cooking apples
(about 1 pound), peeled, cored,
quartered and cut into ¼-inch-
thick slices
5 tablespoons sugar
1 egg

½ cup heavy cream
2 tablespoons flour
1 tablespoon cognac
A 9-inch baked pastry shell *(see
Zwiebelwähe, page 4)*, left in
its false-bottom pan
1 tablespoon water
½ cup apricot preserves

Preheat the oven to 350°. In a deep bowl, combine the apples and 4 tablespoons of the sugar, and turn the slices about with a spoon until they are evenly coated. Beat the egg and cream together with a wire whisk in another bowl for about a minute, then beat in the remaining tablespoon of sugar, the flour and cognac.

Arrange the apple slices attractively in slightly overlapping concentric circles in the baked pastry shell and bake in the middle of the oven for 20 minutes. Then pour in the custard mixture and bake for 15 minutes longer, or until the custard has puffed and browned and a knife inserted in the center comes out clean. Remove from the oven and set aside to cool.

In a small saucepan, combine the water and the preserves, and bring to a simmer over moderate heat, stirring until the preserves dissolve. Then continue to simmer until the mixture thickens to a syrupy glaze. With the back of a spoon, rub the preserves through a fine sieve into a bowl. While the tart is still warm, brush the glaze gently over its entire top surface. Set the false-bottom pan on a large jar or coffee can and slip down the outside rim. Let the tart cool to room temperature and serve.

Makowiec *(Poland)*
CHRISTMAS POPPY-SEED ROLL

To make 1 roll

FILLING
¾ cup black poppy seeds
1 tablespoon unsalted butter
3 tablespoons sugar

3 tablespoons honey
2 tablespoons seedless raisins
¼ cup blanched almonds,
pulverized in a nut grinder or
with a mortar and pestle
1 egg white

Place the poppy seeds in a small heatproof bowl, pour in enough boiling water to cover them by at least 1 inch, and let them soak for 3 hours.

Drain the poppy seeds in a fine sieve and spread them out on paper towels to dry. Then pulverize them in a blender or with mortar and pestle.

In a small skillet, melt 1 tablespoon of butter over moderate heat.

When the foam begins to subside, stir in the poppy seeds, sugar and honey. Reduce the heat to low and, stirring frequently, simmer for about 10 minutes, or until all the liquid in the pan has evaporated and the mixture is thick enough to hold its shape almost solidly in a spoon. With a rubber spatula, scrape the entire contents of the skillet into a deep bowl. Cool to room temperature, then add the raisins and almonds, and stir until well mixed.

Beat the egg white with a wire whisk or a rotary or electric beater until it forms unwavering peaks on the beater when it is lifted from the bowl. Scoop the egg white over the poppy-seed mixture and, with a spatula, fold them together gently but thoroughly. Cover the bowl with foil or plastic wrap and refrigerate for at least 1 hour.

DOUGH

¾ cup lukewarm milk (110° to 115°)	2 tablespoons rum
	½ teaspoon vanilla extract
1 package active dry yeast	1½ teaspoons finely grated fresh
¼ cup confectioners' sugar	orange peel
2¼ cups all-purpose flour	6 tablespoons unsalted butter,
3 egg yolks	softened

To make the dough: Pour the milk into a small bowl and sprinkle it with the yeast and ½ teaspoon of the confectioners' sugar. Let the mixture stand for 2 or 3 minutes, then stir to dissolve the yeast completely. Set the bowl aside in a warm, draft-free place (such as an unlighted oven) for 10 minutes, or until the mixture almost doubles in volume.

Sift 2 cups of the flour and the remaining confectioners' sugar into a deep bowl and make a well in the center. Pour in the yeast mixture, egg yolks, rum and vanilla and, with a large spoon, gradually stir the flour into the liquid ingredients. Continue to stir until well mixed, then stir in the orange peel and beat in the 6 tablespoons of softened butter a few tablespoonfuls at a time. The dough should be just firm enough to be gathered into a ball. If necessary, stir in up to ¼ cup more flour, adding it by the tablespoon.

On a lightly floured surface, knead the dough by pushing it down with the heels of your hands, pressing it forward, and folding it back on itself. Repeat—pushing, pressing and folding—for about 10 minutes, or until the dough is smooth and elastic. Gather it into a ball, place it in a lightly buttered bowl, and dust the top with flour. Drape the bowl with a towel and set it aside in the draft-free place for about 1 hour, or until the dough doubles in volume.

1 tablespoon unsalted butter, softened	1 egg white, lightly beaten
	1 egg, lightly beaten

With a pastry brush, spread 1 tablespoon of softened butter evenly on an 11-by-16-inch jelly-roll pan. Punch the dough down with a single blow

Continued on next page   143

of your fist and, on a lightly floured surface, roll it out into a rectangle about 15 inches long and 10 inches wide and no more than ¼ inch thick. Brush the dough with the beaten egg white and then, with a metal spatula, spread the poppy-seed filling over the surface to within about ½ inch of the edges. Starting at one of the 15-inch-long sides, roll the dough jelly-roll fashion into a tight cylinder. Carefully transfer the roll, seam side down, to the buttered jelly-roll pan. Let it rise in the draft-free place for about 20 minutes, then brush the top and sides of the roll with the beaten egg.

While the roll is rising, preheat the oven to 325°. Bake the *makowiec* in the middle of the oven for about 30 minutes, or until it is a light golden brown. Transfer the roll to a wire cake rack and let it cool to room temperature before slicing and serving.

Kab el Ghzal *(Morocco)*
PASTRY CRESCENTS FILLED WITH ALMOND PASTE ("GAZELLE HORNS")

To make about 40 pastries

PASTRY
1 pound unsalted butter, chilled and
   cut into ¼- inch bits

3 cups all-purpose flour
½ teaspoon salt
6 to 8 tablespoons ice water

In a large chilled bowl, combine the butter bits, flour and salt. With your fingertips, rub the flour and butter together until they look like flakes of coarse meal. Do not let the mixture become oily. Pour 6 tablespoons of ice water over the mixture all at once, toss together lightly, and gather the dough into a ball. If the dough crumbles, add up to 2 tablespoons more ice water by drops until the particles adhere. Divide the dough into halves, dust each half with a little flour, and wrap it in wax paper. Refrigerate for at least 1 hour before using.

ALMOND-PASTE FILLING
½ cup blanched slivered almonds
An 8-ounce can prepared almond
   paste, softened
4 tablespoons unsalted butter,
   softened

1 tablespoon sugar
1 egg
3 tablespoons orange-blossom water
   (see Glossary)
½ cup confectioners' sugar

Meanwhile, preheat the oven to 350°. Spread the almonds out in a shallow baking pan and, turning them occasionally, toast them in the middle of the oven for 8 to 10 minutes, until they are lightly browned. Pulverize the almonds in an electric blender or with a nut grinder or mortar and pestle. Then, with the back of a spoon, rub them through a fine sieve into a deep bowl. Add the almond paste, 4 tablespoons of butter, sugar, egg and 1 tablespoon of the orange-blossom water, and beat vigorously with a spoon until the mixture is smooth.

Raise the oven heat to 400°. On a lightly floured surface, pat half of the dough into a rough rectangle about 1 inch thick. Dust a little flour over and under it, and roll it out from the center to within an inch of the far edge of the pastry. Lift the dough and turn it in the opposite direction; roll again from the center to within an inch or so of the far edge. Repeat—lifting, turning, rolling—until the rectangle is a little less than ⅛ inch thick. If the dough sticks at any point during the rolling, lift it gently with a metal spatula and sprinkle a little flour under it.

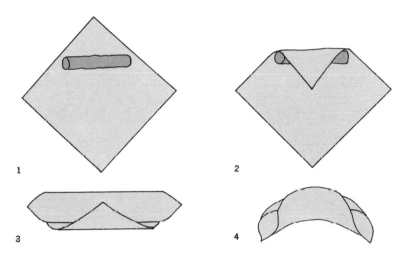

With a ruler and a pastry wheel or a sharp knife, cut the dough into 3-inch squares. For each *kab el ghzal,* roll 1 teaspoon of the almond paste between your palms to make a cylinder about 2 inches long and ½ inch in diameter. Place the cylinder diagonally across one corner of a dough square, about ½ inch from the point *(above, 1),* and lift the point over the paste *(2).* Then, starting with the folded edge, roll the dough up tightly jelly-roll fashion *(3),* tucking in the ends as you proceed. Pinch the ends firmly together and gently shape the pastry roll into a crescent *(4).*

Arrange the crescents about 1 inch apart on an ungreased baking sheet and bake in the middle of the oven for 20 minutes, or until they are golden brown. Transfer the baked *kab el ghzal* to wire cake racks and sprinkle them evenly with 1 tablespoon of orange-blossom water. One at a time, dip the pastries in the confectioners' sugar to coat them lightly, and return them to the racks to cool.

While the first batch of pastries is baking, roll and cut the remaining half of the dough and fill and shape the squares in the identical fashion. While the first batch is cooling, bake the second batch in the middle of the oven for 20 minutes, transfer them to racks and sprinkle them with the rest of the orange-blossom water. Roll in confectioners' sugar and let the pastries cool to room temperature before serving.

Tarte de Quetsches *(Luxembourg)*
PLUM TART WITH CURRANT JELLY

To make one 9-inch tart

PASTRY

1⅓ cups plus 2 tablespoons flour	stick) plus 1 tablespoon unsalted
1 tablespoon sugar	butter, softened
3 egg yolks	2 teaspoons finely grated fresh
8 tablespoons (1 quarter-pound	lemon peel

Combine 1⅓ cups of the flour and the sugar, and sift them into a deep bowl. Make a well in the center, drop in the egg yolks and, stirring gently, gradually incorporate the flour into the yolks. Beat in 8 tablespoons of the softened butter, 1 tablespoon at a time, then add the lemon peel and continue to beat until the dough is smooth and pliable. Gather the dough into a ball, wrap in wax paper, and refrigerate for at least 30 minutes.

With a pastry brush, spread the 1 tablespoon of softened butter evenly over the bottom and sides of a 9-inch false-bottomed fluted quiche pan. Sprinkle 2 tablespoons of flour over the butter and tip the pan from side to side to spread the flour evenly. Invert the pan and rap the bottom sharply to remove the excess flour.

On a lightly floured surface, pat the dough into a circle about 1 inch thick. Dust a little flour over and under it and roll it out into a circle about 13 to 14 inches in diameter and ⅛ inch thick. Drape the dough over the rolling pin, lift it up and unroll it slackly over the prepared pan. Gently press the dough into the bottom and against the sides of the pan. Roll the pin over the rim of the pan, pressing down hard to trim off the excess pastry. Chill the pastry-lined pan for 30 minutes or more.

FILLING	washed, cut lengthwise in half
3 pounds firm ripe plums,	and pitted
preferably Italian damson,	½ cup red or black currant jelly

Preheat the oven to 375°. Arrange the plum halves, cut side up, in concentric circles in the pastry-lined pan. If the plums are small, it may be necessary to arrange them in two layers. Bake in the middle of the oven for 1 hour, or until the tart is brown and the plums are tender.

Remove the tart from the oven, set the pan on a large jar or can and slip down the outside rim. Let cool to room temperature, then run a large metal spatula under the tart to loosen the bottom, and slide the tart off onto a serving plate. Before serving, heat the jelly in a small pan until it melts. With the back of a spoon, rub the jelly through a fine sieve into a small bowl. Then, with a pastry brush, glaze the surface of the plums with the jelly while it is still warm. Set the tart aside to cool to room temperature, but do not refrigerate.

Recipe Index: English

NOTE: Size, weight and material are specified for pans in the recipes because they affect cooking results. A pan should be just large enough to hold its contents comfortably. Heavy pans heat slowly and cook food at a constant rate. Aluminum and cast iron conduct heat well but may discolor foods containing egg yolks, wine, vinegar or lemon. Enamelware is a fairly poor conductor of heat. Many recipes therefore recommend stainless steel or enameled cast iron, which do not have these faults.

Egg and Cheese Dishes

Soups and Accompaniments

Fish and Shellfish

Poultry and Game

Meat

Vegetables and Grains

Meat

egetables and Grains

lads and Relishes

Breads and Brik

Candies and Desserts

Cakes, Pies and Cookies

Glossary

BRYNZA (Romania): A brined white sheep's-milk cheese resembling Greek FETA. Available in cheese stores.

CHAKCHOUKA (Tunisia): A spicy vegetable mixture used as a base in soups or TOUAJEN.

CITRIC, OR SOUR, SALT: A crystalline product extracted from lemons and limes that imparts an acidulous taste, and is used to flavor the jelly that is part of *karp po żydowsku*, Poland's sweet-and-sour carp dish.

COUSCOUS (North Africa): Tiny pastalike pellets usually made with semolina and water. Also the cooked dish of steamed *couscous* with sauce, or other accompaniment.

COUSCOUSSIER (North Africa): A pot like a double boiler with openings like a sieve in the bottom of the top pot. COUSCOUS grains steam uncovered in the top pot, while the accompanying sauce or stew simmers in the bottom pot. Available in specialty cookware stores.

FETA: A Greek cheese. Made from sheep's or goat's milk, it is white and pleasantly pungent. Available in Greek or specialty shops in the United States, it may be substituted for BRYNZA and SIRENE.

FILO: Tissue-thin sheets of pastry that can be purchased fresh or frozen by the pound in Greek or specialty shops. It is used in making BANITSA and may be used as a substitute for MALSOUQUA in BRIK and BASTILA. Should be kept refrigerated. As *filo* dries out instantly, the sheets should be kept covered with a damp towel while being used.

GOUDA (Netherlands): A smooth, mellow cheese made from whole milk, similar in taste and texture to EDAM. Also made in the United States.

HRISA (North Africa): A combination of spices, predominantly crushed red pepper, used to flavor and season almost anything except desserts.

JUNIPER BERRIES: The fruit of the juniper tree, about the size of peppercorns, they are available dried. They have a warm, pungent flavor and are widely used in Belgian cooking.

KASHKAVAL (Romania, Bulgaria): A mild, yellowish table cheese, also used for grating, made from sheep's milk. Available in cheese stores. Provolone or sweet Münster can be substituted.

KIRSCH (Switzerland): A brandy distilled from cherries. Imported brands have a more delicate flavor than domestic United States types.

ORANGE-BLOSSOM WATER (North Africa): An extract of orange blossoms used as a flavoring agent. Available in Middle Eastern or specialty stores.

ORZO: Tiny oval-shaped pasta resembling grains of rice in appearance.

RACLETTE (Switzerland): A melted-cheese dish; also the name of a cheese for making it that is exported to the United States.

ROSE WATER (North Africa): A sweet liquid flavoring distilled from rose petals; the petals are often imported from Bulgaria. Available in Middle Eastern stores or specialty shops.

SALTPETER: A curing agent; used in making KIEŁBASA. Available in drugstores.

SEMOLINA: Finely granulated meal made from the branless inner kernels of durum wheat grains. It is used in the manufacture of pasta and COUSCOUS. Available in Middle Eastern or specialty stores.

Mail-Order Sources

The following stores, grouped by region, accept mail orders for foods called for in this book. Unless the name of the store is self-explanatory, those places that carry cheeses only are so indicated; all other stores listed carry a variety of canned and dried products; a few will ship fresh ones. Because policies differ and managements change, check with the store in question to determine what it has in stock, the current prices, and how best to buy the items you want. Be as specific as possible when inquiring. Some stores require a minimum amount on mail orders, ranging from $2.50 to $25.

East

George Malko
185 Atlantic Ave.
Brooklyn, N.Y. 11201

Sahadi Importing Co., Inc.
187 Atlantic Ave.
Brooklyn, N.Y. 11201

Kalustyan Orient Export Trading
Corp.
123 Lexington Ave.
New York, N.Y. 10016

European Grocery Store
520 Court Pl.
Pittsburgh, Pa. 15219

Stamoolis Bros. Grocery
2020 Penn Ave.
Pittsburgh, Pa. 15222

Cheese & Wine Cellar
Montgomery Mall
Bethesda, Md. 20034

Wine & Cheese Shop
1413 Wisconsin Ave., N.W.
Washington, D.C. 20007

Acropolis Food Market
1206 Underwood St., N.W.
Washington, D.C. 20015

Magruder's Grocers
5626 Connecticut Ave., N.W.
Washington, D.C. 20015

South

Hickory Farms Inc. (cheeses)
2030 Lawrenceville Highway
Decatur, Ga. 30033

Antone's Import Co.
P.O. Box 3352
(807 Taft St.)
Houston, Tex. 77019

Barzizza Brothers International
Trade Center
351 So. Front St.
Memphis, Tenn. 38103

Bert's Groceteria
3464 Main Highway
Miami, Fla. 33133

Progress Grocery
915 Decatur St.
New Orleans, La. 70116

Ideal Bakery *(filo)*
2436 Ursulines Ave.
New Orleans, La. 70119

Midwest

Swiss Colony
Lindale Plaza
Cedar Rapids, Iowa 52402

Conte-Di-Savoia
555 W. Roosevelt Rd.
Chicago, Ill. 60607

Shiekh Grocery (cheeses)
652 Bolivar Rd.
Cleveland, Ohio 44115

Samos Wholesale Grocery (cheeses)
727 Bolivar Rd.
Cleveland, Ohio 44115

Demmas Shish-Ke-Bob
5806 Hampton Ave.
St. Louis, Mo. 63109

Heidi's Around the World Food
Shop
1149 So. Brentwood Blvd.
St. Louis, Mo. 63117

Paul's Cheese Stall
116 Union Market
St. Louis, Mo. 63101

West

Economy Domestic and Imported
Grocery
973 Broadway
Denver, Colo. 80203

C & K Importing Co.
2771 West Pico Blvd.
Los Angeles, Calif. 90006

Haig's
441 Clement St.
San Francisco, Calif. 94118

Vern Anderson's Delicatessen
9575 S.W. Beaverton Highway
Beaverton, Ore. 97005

De Laurenti Importing
Stall 5, Lower Pike Place Market
Seattle, Wash. 98101

Canada

Main Importing Co., Inc.
1188 St. Lawrence
Montreal 126, Quebec

Cooke's Fine Foods
5961 Brock St.
Kingston, Ontario

The Cheese Shop
258 Laurier Ave. West
Ottawa 4, Ontario

Notes

Illustrations on pages 2, 10, 26, 38, 54, 85, 98, 105, 114, 127
by David Palladini. Diagrams on pages 7, 19, 111, 126, 145
by Gloria duBouchet. All photographs by Richard Jeffery except page 68 by Fred Eng.

x